Biology Help for the Virtual Weary Student

17 Stories to ace the tests, pass the class, and finally understand

Written by:

Heather Moran

For Halle and Albert
And all the students who have helped me
craft the stories throughout the years

Contents

INTRODUCTION

Welcome to the wonderful world of biology!

During the pandemic of 2020, I was talking with a parent who was trying to help her son with his online biology course. She said, "We have the textbook, we have a workbook, and we have an answer key. So, we know that the answer to the question is 'mitosis,' but we have no idea why. We just don't understand *why* that is the answer or what it is we are supposed to be learning. It feels like a useless exercise and it's all just very frustrating. We need someone to explain and break this down for us."

Ah, my friend, you need a teacher! I am a biology teacher. I'm also a parent and a lifelong enthusiast of science.

I've always felt that it was my job, as a secondary science teacher, to translate the often "gobbly-goo" jargon of scientific papers into simple, understandable concepts. I strive to bring the wonder and, yes, *joy* into grappling with the questions and mysteries of life. "Bios" = "life" and "ology" = "study of." And truly, for those of us who have the good fortune to be alive, what can be more important than the *study of life*?

Whether you are an online biology student, a parent trying to help a biology student, or any learner who just wants to have a better comprehension of biology, I hope these stories help and inspire you. The 17 stories in this book cover some of the most important concepts in biology. These are the major concepts that will carry you through all other biology courses. They will also be the most "tested" concepts, preparing you for any standardized test from state graduation requirements to college entrance exams. This book is in no way, nor is it meant to be, a comprehensive study of biology. The world of biology is large and complex and has many paths for further study. My hope is that this book will be a companion to you and shed extra light on your first steps through that path.

I almost always start my lectures with, "When last we left the wonderful world of biology…" because it truly is a wonderful world.

So, welcome to the wonderful world of biology!

STORY #1: YOUR JEANS ARE DEAD
(WHAT IS LIFE?)

What is Life?

Biology is the study of life. In order to study life, we first need to figure out what is living. At first, this seems pretty easy: A frog is living. A rock is not. But what about a cloud, a virus, the sun, water, your jeans? What determines life? This is not an easy question, not even for scientists.

To figure out what is living, **I usually have my students go outside and list 50–100 things that we will then categorize. I tell them that when they get stuck, they can look very large (the sky!) or very small (an ant!). There are usually one or two students that list things like bacteria, oxygen, and the universe – and I never said they couldn't! It's okay, it makes for interesting discussions. We then put these things into one of three categories; living, never living, and dead. Pick any of the three categories to start. You picked dead – morbid.**

Dead

<u>**Okay. Your jeans are dead. Why? They came from cotton (we assume) and cotton was once a living plant. And now it is dead. Your house is made of wood, so it is also dead. Papers, pencils (at least wooden pencils) are dead. Your parents bought you dead jeans and dead school supplies. Great.**</u>

At some point we usually encounter something plastic (let's say a plastic pencil). This is good. Plastic comes from the refining of oil. Oil is a fossil fuel (that's a sciency term), it comes from dead and decaying plants and animals from millions of years ago. So, technically, plastic is dead. Most people say that plastic is never living, but you could argue that it is dead.

Never Living

Things that are made of metal, glass, and rocks (like bricks) are never living. (Although sand and the production of glass can be an interesting side discussion here.)

Living

Birds, bacteria, humans (we hope), ants, etc., are living.

Tricky Ones

Some things are tricky to categorize, and that's where it gets fun.

Clouds: Imagine a cloud. Then it splits in two. Did it reproduce? Isn't that how bacteria reproduce (binary fission)? Clouds move. They use energy. They change in response to their environment. Living?!

The sun: The sun has cells (convection cells), it moves, it responds to the environment. Stars can grow and they certainly use energy. Living?!

<u>Six Characteristics of Life</u>

Every biology course starts with a discussion of the **Characteristics of Life.** I've seen lists with 5, 6, 7, even 10 characteristics of life. We'll use 6. The thought process is the same with any of the lists: To find out whether a thing is living, we check whether it has all the characteristics on the list.

1. Cells (in the biological sense)
2. Organization
3. Energy Use
4. Homeostasis (that's a sciency word!)
5. Growth (by cell division and cell enlargement)
6. Reproduction

If we look at our cloud, we can say that it is organized (storm clouds at least organize positive and negative charges), uses energy, undergoes homeostasis, grows and reproduces. So, is it living? No. A cloud does not have cells in the biological sense[1]. (You know – **cell: a membrane-bound structure that is the basic unit of life**.) So, clouds are not living.

Also, clouds grow by accumulating more of the stuff they are made of (mostly dust and water vapor). Living things grow by cell division and cell enlargement: they have cells that undergo **mitosis**. Clouds do *not* have cells that undergo **mitosis** – that is another reason they cannot be considered living.

A note on reproduction: Reproduction must take place within the species if the species is to continue. However, it is not essential that each individual reproduce for it to be considered living. This is usually a great relief to my students.

More things that are never living: icicles, fire, stars (including the sun) and water. Water can be *in* living things. Water can also have living things *in it*. However, water itself is never living.

There are things that are even trickier to categorize. Take soil, for example: Soil is most often defined as a mixture of organic matter, minerals, gases, liquids, and organisms

---

[1] Clouds do not have those biological cells; clouds only have *convection cells*.

that together support life. So, soil is a mixture of never living (minerals), dead (leaves, ants, manure), and living (bacteria, fungus, worms).We could go further and discuss if manure is living, never living, or dead, but that is a rather crappy discussion[2].

What about bacteria? Bacteria are single-celled, but that one cell that they have is enough. They are also organized, use energy, respond to their environment, grow (by cell division and cell enlargement), and can reproduce. Bacteria are living.

What about viruses? Let's run the list. Viruses can certainly reproduce, but only when they are inside other cells. Viruses do use energy, respond to their environment, and are organized. However, viruses are not cells. They contain DNA or RNA, but are not a complete cell. Since viruses do not have even one cell, they cannot grow by cell division or enlargement. Viruses are not living.

This was a conundrum to scientists. Obviously, studying viruses is an important thing for scientists to do. But in order to function, scientists need to **define and classify** things (it's what we do). So, science made up a definition for viruses. (See the Sciency Words list below.)

In conclusion: in order to effectively study biology, one needs to know what life is. When we think of life, we most often think of ourselves, humans. Perhaps we think about other animals or even plants. However, we must think about life in its more basic form. What makes life? What is it that ties all living things together? Why is it that some life is a redwood tree, and some life is a giant squid, and some life is you?

Welcome to the wonderful world of biology!

---

[2] Science teacher jokes are legendary! I will continue, as my gift to you. You are welcome!

Sciency words

Virus – a nonliving, infectious, biological particle composed of a nucleic acid and a protein coat.

Fossil Fuel – a natural fuel such as coal or gas, formed in the geological past from the remains of living organisms.

Binary Fission – asexual reproduction by a separation of the body into two new bodies.

Convection Cell – A convection cell is a system in which a fluid is warmed, loses density, and is forced into a region of greater density. The cycle repeats and a pattern of motion forms. Convection cells in Earth's atmosphere are responsible for the blowing of wind, and they can be found in a variety of other natural and manmade phenomena.

Homeostasis – the ability to maintain a relatively stable internal state that persists despite changes in the world outside. (Body temperature up > sweating > body temperature down. Blood sugar up > insulin released > blood sugar down.)

Mitosis – cellular process where a single cell divides resulting in two identical cells.

STORY #2: BAKING IS EASY TO UNDERSTAND BECAUSE COOKIES ARE DELICIOUS – PART 1 (CHEMISTRY FOR BIOLOGY STUDENTS)

Chemistry for Life

Chemistry is complicated. It is. There's the Periodic Table of Elements, and it lists around 119 elements, and scientists are always finding new elements. There are a lot of numbers and symbols and things to memorize and aarrgghh. It's complicated. Is the Periodic Table of the Elements really important? Is there any way to make it understandable? Is there a story? Yes. Yes. And yes.

Let's say you love baking. You walk into your dream kitchen. The kitchen is well stocked with everything you can ever dream of to bake with. Of course, you have the main ingredients of baking; flour, sugar, butter, eggs – you will use these in almost everything you bake. Then you have other ingredients you may use often; brown sugar, salt, vanilla extract, baking soda. Your dream kitchen has a lot of other ingredients too, though, like walnuts, chocolate, strawberries, cheese, peanut butter, ginger, corn, peaches, tomato sauce, and hundreds of other ingredients! How can you keep them organized? What about some sort of chart? Do you see where I'm going with this?

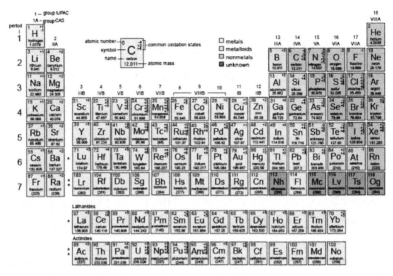

See, some ingredients go together really well (like peanut butter and chocolate). Others do NOT go together at all (like peanut butter and tomato sauce – yuck!). Other ingredients are best enjoyed by themselves – they really shouldn't be combined at all. Elements are the same way. The Periodic Table of Elements organizes the elements based on how well they combine with one another, along with other characteristics about the elements.

For example, each atom of sodium (Na) has a charge of +1. That is because they usually lose one electron in their outermost energy level. Each atom of chloride (Cl) has a charge of -1. That is because they usually pick up one electron in their outermost energy level. They come together perfectly, *like chocolate and peanut butter.* It's not only these two elements that go well together. ALL the elements in Column 1 lose an electron and become +1, just like Sodium (Na+). ALL the elements in Column 17 gain an electron and become -1, just like Chloride (Cl-). So, even though these columns are found on different sides of the table, they combine often. The Periodic Table lists the elements in a way that shows this. It really is super important and super enjoyable. This is the foundation of chemistry.

Consider an element like neon. Neon is stable in its outermost energy level. It has an atomic number of 10. That means it has 10 protons and, as long as it is neutral (and it will be neutral for all of this discussion), it also has 10 electrons. The first energy level can hold 2 electrons, and it is full with 2 electrons. The second energy level can hold 8 electrons, and it is full with 8 electrons. 2 + 8 = 10. (I know you knew that, but it's nice to have an easy one thrown at you.) Let's take a look at neon:

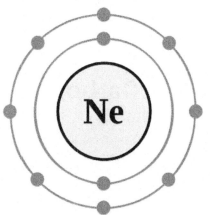

See. It's stable. Neon is usually found on its own. This is why you hear about sodium chloride, but you would never hear about neon chloride. Neon (and all of the noble gases) are only found by themselves in nature. They do not combine naturally. The Periodic Table shows that the noble gases are similar by grouping them together.

Back to Biology

"This is supposed to help me with biology, not chemistry,"
you may be thinking. True. Let's get back to it. Are some ele-
ments more important than others? In biology, yes! Just like
in baking (flour, sugar, butter, eggs), life is built with four
major elements. Those four elements are carbon, oxygen, hy-
drogen, and nitrogen.

Carbon is the main building block of life. We are all carbon-
based life forms. Carbon has an atomic number of 6. That
means it has 6 protons (positively charged subatomic particles). Assuming that carbon is neutral (and we will for the
duration of this discussion), that means carbon also has 6
electrons (negatively charged subatomic particles). Let's
look at an atom of carbon.

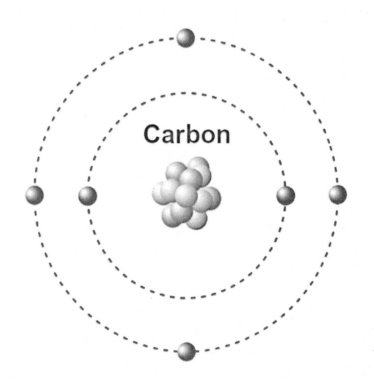

The first energy level can hold 2 electrons. In carbon, it is full with 2 electrons. The second energy level can hold 8 electrons. In carbon, it is holding only 4 electrons. That means for carbon to be stable, it would like to SHARE 4 more electrons in order to make the second energy level full. (I use the word SHARE because this is what carbon tends to do.) This sharing of electrons forms a **covalent bond** in chemistry. Because carbon is always looking to share electrons, it forms bonds easily. The elements that carbon most often shares bonds with are other carbons, hydrogen, and oxygen. Quite often carbon bonds with nitrogen as well.

Let's look at carbon doing its thing!

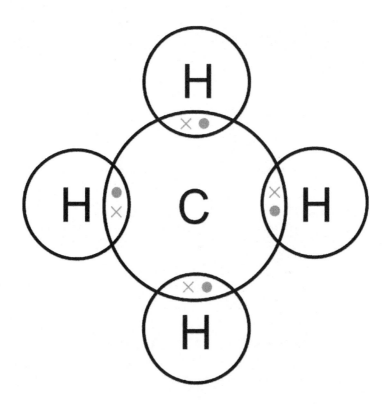

This is methane. It's a gas you might use to heat your home. See how carbon is sharing electrons with 4 hydrogen atoms? This makes carbon stable, and it makes the hydrogens stable as well. Methane is the simplest organic compound.

The Chemistry of Carbon is the Chemistry of Life!

There is a whole branch of chemistry dedicated to carbon! It is called organic chemistry. Organic chemistry is the basis for fossil fuels, agriculture, and all of life. So … pretty important.

Carbon (along with hydrogen, oxygen, nitrogen, and occasionally some of those other elements) make up *carbohydrates*, *proteins*, *fats (lipids)*, and *nucleic acids*. Those 4 things make up all of life, and they are called **macromolecules**. Let's look at them:

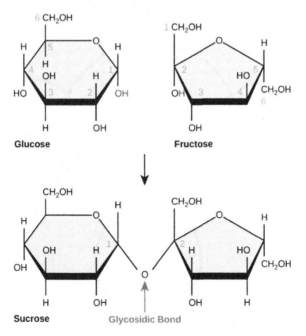

Simple carbohydrates. Chemistry style.

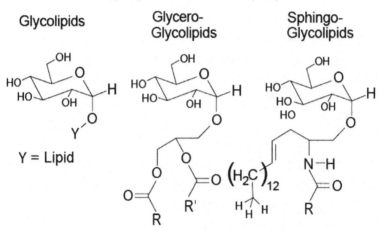

Simple protein. Chemistry style.

Glycolipids

Glycero-Glycolipids

Sphingo-Glycolipids

Y = Lipid

Simple fat (lipid). Chemistry style.

Nucleic Acid. If you study **biochemistry**,
this is a lot of what you will be studying.

The point I'm trying to make with these rather complicated diagrams is that **all of life is made up of carbon, hydrogen, oxygen, and nitrogen.** The other elements are sometimes added in. For example, you can see that phosphate (see the "P" on the left-hand side of the diagram) is an ingredient in nucleic acids. All of life, including you, is built with carbohydrates, fats (lipids), proteins, and nucleic acids. These 4 macromolecules are built with carbon, hydrogen, oxygen, and nitrogen.

- Elements make up macromolecules.
- Macromolecules make up life.
- C, H, O, and N make up carbohydrates, proteins, fats (lipids), and nucleic acids.
- Carbohydrates, proteins, fats (lipids), and nucleic acids make up life.

How do they build life? Next essay!

Sciency Words

Covalent bond – the linkage that results from two atoms sharing an electron pair.

Organic chemistry – the scientific study of the structures, properties, compositions, reactions, and syntheses of **organic compounds**.

Organic compounds – molecules that are *always* composed of carbon and hydrogen (they may also contain any number of other elements).

Biochemistry – the scientific study of the chemical substances and processes that occur in plants, animals, and microorganisms and of the changes they undergo during development and life.

Story #3: Building Your Dream Home (Macromolecules)

Building Life: Macromolecules

Let's say you are about to build your dream home. What do you need? Well, you need the plan, or blueprint. You need different workers that look at your blueprint and then do the work to their specifications. You need the building materials (bricks, beams, windows, toilets, door locks, etc.). And you need money – lots of it! Money to pay the workers, money to run the equipment, money to purchase supplies, and money in the bank in case something goes wrong.

To build living things (trees, whales, mushrooms, humans) you need these things as well:

- Plans (Blueprint) – **DNA** (deoxyribonucleic acid)
- Workers – **RNA** (ribonucleic acid)
- Building materials – **proteins**
- Energy/Money – **carbohydrates**

Fats (lipids) are quite neat: they are used as building materials (they are a major component of the **cell membrane**), they are burned as energy, AND any extra fats can be stored for later use (money in the bank).

In the last lesson, we talked about how elements (mostly carbon, oxygen, hydrogen, and nitrogen) make up the four macromolecules. These molecules are called "macro" because living things need them in large amounts.

Let's look at what each of the macromolecules do. This is an overview, all these things will be discussed in more detail later.

NUCLEIC ACIDS

DNA (Deoxyribonucleic Acid)

This is found in almost every cell in your body. Your DNA is the blueprint for *you*. Your DNA tells how tall you are going to be, what color your eyes are, if any genetic disorders are present, what your hair looks like, and what sort of digestive enzymes you produce. It is the genetic book of you! It is a recipe book for anything about you that is controlled by genetics.

Biologists know exactly how to read some parts of DNA. For example, by doing a DNA test, biologists can tell if you have Down's syndrome, sickle cell anemia, your gender, and what sort of ear wax you have, among many, many other things.

However, there are some parts of DNA that we don't know how to read yet. Biologists are still working on that and there is still a lot of work to be done. It seems like heart disease, some cancers, and even alcoholism may have a genetic component, but science is still at work!

You may remember that there are two main types of cells; **prokaryote** and **eukaryote** (more sciency words). Animal and plant cells are eukaryotes. That means they have a nucleus. The nucleus is where the DNA is stored in eukaryotic cells. The DNA does not leave the nucleus!

At any rate, DNA is in practically every cell in your body (except for red blood cells: they do not have a nucleus). **The recipe for all of you is in every single one of your cells!** Your hair follicle cells have the recipe in them for making digestive enzymes. And your pancreas cells, in addition to recipes for digestive enzymes, have the recipe for making your hair! That seems sort of crazy. We do not want our pancreas to start making hair! And yet, it has the recipe to do so. DNA – the blueprint for how to make a human (or frog, or mushroom) – is written in almost every cell in that organism, whether or not that cell uses all of the information.

RNA (Ribonucleic Acid)

There are different types of RNA. I will now be talking about mRNA – that stands for messenger RNA. It is the number one type of RNA you should know about. We'll get to some others later.

Remember that the DNA does not leave the nucleus? *It's like Grandma's golden family cookbook – it never leaves the kitchen!* So how does the rest of the cell get the recipe to make, let's say, insulin? Insulin is a digestive enzyme (protein) made by the pancreas. If you've just eaten a candy bar (carbohydrate), you're going to need some extra insulin (protein) to take all that extra sugar (carbohydrate) to storage.

It is the mRNA's job to enter the nucleus, open the DNA to the correct recipe for insulin, copy that recipe, close the DNA, then take the copy of the recipe for insulin out of the nucleus and into the **ribosomes**. The ribosomes will then read the recipe and make the insulin.

I explain it to my students like this:

Say you want to make Grandma's brownies for movie night over at your friend Ralph's house. You are planning on taking Grandma's golden family cookbook over to Ralph's house, but Grandma says, "No way! The golden family cookbook does not leave the kitchen!" **DNA does not leave the nucleus of the eukaryotic cell.** *So, you go into the kitchen, open the cookbook to just the right page, take a picture of* *the recipe, close the cookbook, and exit the kitchen.* **You are** **acting like mRNA.** *You then take the recipe to Ralph's kitchen (***ribosome***) and prepare the brownies (*insulin – or whatever protein the living thing needs*).*

PROTEINS

Proteins are the building blocks of living things. Your hair is a protein. Insulin is a protein. Your skin is a protein. Your muscles are proteins. The shape of proteins is very important. If the shape of a protein is not correct, the protein will not work. Proteins are building materials. If the shape of the window, door, lock, or toilet in your house is incorrect, then that building material will not work. If the shape of your protein is not correct, then whatever that protein does will not be correct. For example: In the genetic disease cystic fibrosis, a protein is made incorrectly (or in some cases not at all). This misshapen protein causes the person's mucus to be too thick. This causes major problems for the lungs and other organs.

Proteins are made up of **amino acids.** *Back in preschool, you used all sorts of colorful building blocks to build all sorts of castles. Each building block had a different color and shape and they came together in all sorts of incredible buildings.* There are **20 different amino acids.** Each protein is made of 20–3,000 of these amino acids, and they come together in all sorts of incredible proteins.

Is all this biology talk making you hungry?! Me too! Go eat some chicken, hamburger, or peanut butter. Those are all proteins! Your digestive system will break the chicken down into proteins, and then further into amino acids. Those amino acids will be transported by your blood to your muscle cells. Your muscle cells will take in those amino acids and turn them into proteins (like **actin** and

22

myosin). Proteins make up your muscles. You just turned the chicken's muscles into your own muscles! Weird but also true!

CARBOHYDRATES

Carbohydrates are your energy source.

- Carbohydrates can be simple (glucose, fructose, galactose). The simple ones are called **monosaccharides** ("one sugar").
- Carbohydrates can be double (sucrose – table sugar – yum!). The double ones are called **disaccharides** ("two sugars").
- Carbohydrates can also be bigger (starch, cellulose, glycogen). The bigger ones are called **polysaccharides** ("many sugars").

Carbohydrates are to be burned for energy, like the fuel for a bonfire. Polysaccharides are like the big logs you use at a bonfire – they are harder to break down and can burn for a long time. Disaccharides are like smaller branches. Monosaccharides are more like wood chips or newspaper, they burn quick and hot and then die out quickly.

Carbohydrates all serve the same purpose: they are the power source to give living things their energy. The types of carbohydrates you eat and how they are burned is the source of much research into nutrition and athletics. We know that the carbohydrates in leafy greens (cellulose) burn in a much different way than the carbohydrates in candy (sucrose). As we learn more about how cells utilize carbohydrates, we learn more about good nutrition!

FATS (LIPIDS)

Fats are used to make up the cell membrane. They are also used for long term energy storage (like the money in the bank). When your cells need energy, they will first burn the monosaccharide (glucose) that is in your blood. Next, the cells will burn **glycogen.** That is a type of polysaccharide (remember: "many sugars" so it's a carbohydrate). Glycogen is stored in your liver and muscles. The last place that the cells will get fuel is from fat.

- Blood glucose (carbohydrate) = $5 in your back pocket. Easy to get to and easy to spend. Burned quickly; comes from food you recently ate.
- Glycogen (carbohydrate) = $20 at home in your desk. Took you a little while to save; a little harder to get to; it takes a little longer to burn. Comes from food you ate a while ago.
- Fat (lipid) = the college fund your grandparents started for you. Harder to get to; last place the cell will go for energy. Comes from extra food you've been eating for weeks or longer.

Sciency Words

Cell Membrane – the semipermeable membrane surrounding the cytoplasm of a cell.

Eukaryote – type of cell that has a nucleus and membrane-bound organelles. Animal and plant cells are eukaryotes.

Prokaryote – type of cell that does not have a nucleus and membrane-bound organelles.

Ribosomes – site for protein synthesis in a cell. (They make protein.)

Amino acids – these combine to form proteins.

Actin and Myosin – these proteins create muscle contraction.

STORY #4: TREMENDOUS GINORMOUS SQUID (CELLS & CELL THEORY)

Since about second or third grade, you've been hearing about cells in your science courses. You've had to draw cells, look at differences between plant and animal cells, maybe make models of cells. Yes, you know cells. However, after the science class is over, you never hear about these things again. So why are they so important? What's the big deal about cells?

First let me give you a little history. Back in 1665, **Robert Hooke** (British), was looking at cork (dead plant) under a magnifying device. He discovered that cork was made of repeating units. These repeating units were square and small and he thought they resembled the "cells" that monks slept in – tiny, square, repeating rooms. So, he called them "cells."

Later, in 1674, **Anton van Leuwenhoek** (who is given credit for inventing the first microscope), was using his microscope to look at all sorts of things – things such as pepper, his own teeth scraping, hay, and pond water. He diagrammed and described everything in his notebooks. During his studies, he discovered that some small cells that he saw were living. He called those cells "animalcules" – half animal/half molecule. We now call those cells "bacteria" (however, there are some living cells that are not bacteria, we call those "protists").

Now that the microscope was invented, many scientists started studying the wonderful world of really small life, including the cell. Let's jump forward 165 years, to around

1839. Matthias Schleiden, Theodor Schwann, and Rudolf Virchow pulled together their work (and the work of many others during that time period) into what we now know as the **cell theory**. The cell theory has 3 parts.

Cell Theory

1. All living things are made of cells

2.The cell is the basic unit of structure and function of living things.

3.Cells only come from pre-existing cells.

The cell theory is a basis for biology.We still very much use it today.

1. All Living Things Are Made of Cells

Remember when we were asking if clouds or fire could be considered alive? The answer was no because they do not have cells. However, humans have cells. Dogs, ducks, lettuce, carrots, mushrooms, earthworms, fish, and grass all have cells. There are some small differences between these cells, but they are still remarkably alike!

- All cells have a cell membrane. That membrane is made of proteins and lipids.
- All eukaryotic cells have a nucleus. The nucleus is where the DNA is kept.
- All eukaryotic cells have mRNA that comes into the nucleus, opens the DNA, copies a recipe for protein, and takes that recipe to the ribosomes.
- All cells have ribosomes that make protein.

Imagine the surprise of those early scientists who discovered that our human cells were almost identical to an earthworm's cells! They must have run around, picking up all sorts of living things to test them! Rabbit cells? Yes! Onion cells? Yes! Fish cells? Turnip cells? Eagle cells? Yes, yes, yes! All of life is built out of the same thing, and that is pretty awesome. Humbling, yes, but awesome nonetheless.

This also makes some aspects of biology very **predictable**. Predictability is one of the things scientists look for to contribute to a strong theory (like the cell theory). Let me explain what I mean.

The Predictability of a Tremendous Ginormous Squid

Say that right now, off the coast of Japan, researchers are bringing onto their boat the largest squid ever to be seen by humans. It is a newly discovered species. We will call it the Tremendous Ginormous Squid (why not?). No human has ever seen the Tremendous Ginormous Squid. Ever. It has lived miles beneath the ocean at the bottom of a trench. We have no idea what it eats or how many exist. Scientists from all over the world flock to Japan to get a glimpse of this new and wonderful creature. The Tremendous Ginormous Squid is all over the news. A new species and it's huge! Everyone is talking about it! And yet...

... as a biologist, I'm already a bit bored with it. I mean, I know that it will have cells. They will be eukaryotic animal cells with a cell membrane. The cell membranes will be made of proteins and lipids. (And remember: proteins and lipids are made of carbon, hydrogen, oxygen, and nitrogen.) The squid will have DNA. The DNA will be in the nucleus. Yawn.

Our squid is just another example that cell theory works. It's a tremendous animal, for sure. But it is an animal and we already know how animals work.

Now, if the Tremendous Ginormous Squid is *not* made up of cells, then that is **truly exciting**! We would have to change the cell theory! The one that's been in place since 1839! What if our Tremendous Ginormous Squid were made of crystallized pellets or marshmallow rice treats? That would be life changing! Literally! We'd have to change all the rules!

This will probably not happen. That is why the first part of the cell theory (all living things are made of cells) will probably stand the test of time. And it is why you need to know about cells. Cells make up life; cells make up everything that is alive. And you are alive. And that is awesome!

2. The Cell Is the Basic Unit of Structure and Function of Living Things

Cells cannot get too big. This is because things like oxygen have to squeeze through (diffuse through) the cell membrane. When a cell gets too big, it goes through mitosis and forms a new cell. Biologists are still learning how and why they do this. However, a cell cannot "add on" to itself. It is the basic unit by definition. In a complicated life form, like a human, cells can and do specialize (muscle cells, brain cells, etc.). However, the basic cell is still the basic unit. Elephant cells are the same size as ant cells. Elephants just have **more** cells than ants.

In the same sense, nothing can be alive if it is not a complete cell. DNA by itself is not a living thing. Cell components (**organelles**) are not living things. Viruses contain DNA or RNA and often a protein or ribosomes, but the cell is not complete in viruses. Viruses have ingredients for life, but they are not living things. The cell is the basic unit of structure and function.

3. Cells Only Come from Pre-existing Cells

This means that life only comes from life. No spontaneous generation. Everything has a parent (or something equivalent). Salamanders are not "born in fire." Maggots do not come from rotting meat. Frogs do not come from stone. Fish do not come from mud – yes, fish have to come from mommy and daddy fish. Even bacteria have to come from a parent bacterial cell.

This was big stuff in 1839. Spontaneous generation was all the rage. Most folks, lacking a microscope, really believed that maggots came from rotting meat. Spontaneous generation also tied in nicely with the accepted religious views in Europe at the time.

There is a dilemma here. If life only comes from other life, then where did the first life come from? Answer that question and the scientific world will come running to you (and hopefully drop a lot of money at your feet)! Scientists have been trying to answer that question for a very long time. And yet, in all the time we have been studying life, no one has been able to produce "life" out of "not life." And so, the third and final part of the cell theory stands. Cells only come from pre-existing cells.

Eukaryotic vs. Prokaryotic Cells

Eukaryotic cells have a nucleus and membrane-bound organelles. Animals, plants, fungi, and most protists are all eukaryotic.

Prokaryotic cells do not have a nucleus nor membrane-bound organelles. They have a cell membrane, often a cell wall and outer capsule, often flagella and/or cilia, and ribosomes. They have DNA, but it is not enclosed in a nucleus, it just floats about in the cell. Prokaryotes are single-celled. They include bacteria (all bacteria, good and bad) and a group called archaea. Archaea are the most primitive forms of life and are found in salt lakes, deep thermal vents, geysers, and other ancient Earth-like places.

Animal vs. Plant Cells

Plant cells are quite rigid and box-like. They have a cell wall outside of the cell membrane, which gives the plants more support than animal cells (but less ability to move).

Plants also have chloroplasts and other pigment rich organelles. These capture sunlight (usually) and transfer that energy into chemical energy (food). This is an amazing process called **photosynthesis** (more on that later). Plant cells are usually **larger in size** than animal cells. Plant cells usually have a **very large vacuole** (up to 98% of the cell!) to store water and salts – animal cells instead have several much smaller vacuoles. It is important that plant cells have the ability to store water as most plants cannot move around to find water.

Animal cells are less rigid than plant cells. They lack a cell wall, chloroplasts, and a large vacuole. They are usually smaller in size and do not have the box-like appearance. They often have many more **lysosomes** than plant cells. Lysosomes are organelles that digest waste material for a cell. **Centrioles** are only found in animal cells. Centrioles aid in cellular division (mitosis and meiosis) in animal cells.

Little Stories to Help Remember the Cell Organelles – the Cells' "Organs"

Mitochondria – the mitochondria turn sugar (glucose) into energy (ATP – adenosine triphosphate). Everyone knows that the mitochondrion is "the powerhouse of the cell," but what the heck does that mean? It is the bonfire: It takes carbohydrates (the logs and twigs on the fire) and turns them into energy (light and heat from the bonfire). The energy source that runs living things is **ATP (adenosine triphosphate)**. You should memorize that. It is important. And also, people are impressed when you can say it.

Ribosome – the word ribosome starts with "rib." If you eat **rib**s for dinner, you are eating meat. Meat gives you protein. **Rib**s are protein (and also fat, but ignore that for now). **Rib**osomes make protein.

Ribosomes make protein! **Rib**osomes make protein! **Rib**osomes make protein!

Endoplasmic Reticulum (ER) – **ER** also stands for Emergency Room, so think of the hospital! If you are in the hospital, they put you in a hospital gown and put you on a hospital gurney. They may wheel you down the hall to have an x-ray. They may wheel you upstairs to a room. They **transport** you all over the hospital. They do *not* take you outside and down the street on a hospital gurney in a hospital gown. The **endoplasmic reticulum** is for **internal transportation** within the cell. While in the hospital, they may also regulate your calcium levels and break down some toxic substances. The endoplasmic reticulum does this as well.

Golgi apparatus – the Golgi apparatus packages protein and gets it ready to leave the cell. If you are going to leave the hospital, they will package you differently. You will put on your regular street clothes. You will be put in a car.

If you bake an apple pie in your kitchen, the mRNA is the copy of the recipe. Your kitchen is the ribosome. Your house is the cell. The apple pie is the protein. If you are packaging the apple pie to take to Grandma, who is sitting in the living room (in the same house), you package it a certain way. You probably put it on a plate, with a fork and a napkin. That is what the ER (endoplasmic reticulum) does: it packages a protein for use in the cell. *If you are then packaging the rest of the pie to send to Grandpa in Iceland, you will package it very differently. You will cover the pie with wrap, put it in a box, put foam around it, and address it, tape it, etc.* This is what the **Golgi apparatus** does: it gets proteins ready to **leave the cell**. Because these proteins will be traveling in the bloodstream, they must be packaged differently. They even need to be "addressed" correctly to arrive at their intended spot.

For example, growth hormone is produced in your pituitary gland. This gland is located at the base of your brain. Growth hormone is a protein produced by pituitary cells. For the growth hormone to do its job, it must be packaged by the Golgi apparatus and sent into the bloodstream. The hormone is packaged in a way that allows it to travel in the bloodstream until it gets to the end of long bones (like your femur or humerus). When it gets to the right location, the packaging "fits" into special grooves in the outer membrane of the bone cells. This allows for growth. Cool, huh?

Lysosomes – contain enzymes that digest old organelles. They also digest bacteria and viruses that may enter a cell. They are round and sometimes resemble Pac-man. This is good because they do exactly what Pac-man does: Engulf stuff and get rid of it.

Cilia and Flagella – found on the outside of the cell, these are used in movement. Cilia are smaller and hairlike. They line the inside of your throat (found on the outside of the throat cells) and help to move mucus and dust that may get caught there. Flagella are longer and tail-like. They move the cell. An example in humans is the sperm cell, it has to travel far and move fast.

Nucleus – the home of DNA during normal, eukaryotic cell life.

Vacuole – storage, mostly storing water and salt. In plant cells the vacuoles are large, in animal cells they are smaller.

Plastid – (Most notable: Chloroplast) – contains pigment for photosynthesis or chemosynthesis. More on that later!

Sciency Word

ATP (adenosine triphosphate) – the energy source that runs living things. Created from carbohydrates by the mitochondria.

Story #5: The Best Party Ever (Passive & Active Transport) A story of how things get into and out of a cell.

First of all, why do things need to get into and out of the cell? To maintain **homeostasis**, of course. Also, to keep you alive. For example:

- You eat, and nutrients (proteins, carbohydrates, lipids) end up in your blood.
- You breathe, and oxygen ends up in your blood.
- Harmful bacteria may enter your body.
- A cell has some waste material it needs to get rid of.

Things constantly need to get in and out of the cell. However, not everything is allowed to enter and leave the cell. The cell membrane (made of proteins and lipids) is said to be **selectively permeable**. That means it only allows certain things to enter and leave the cell. Which things? It all depends on what that cell may need at the time.

There are two main categories of how molecules get into and out of your cells; passive transport and active transport. Passive transport uses **no energy from the cell.** Active transport uses **a lot of energy from the cell.**

- In passive transport, molecules move from an area of greater concentration to an area of lesser concentration (*with* their **concentration gradient)**. This requires no energy.
- In active transport, molecules move from an area of lesser concentration to an area of greater concentration (*against* their **concentration gradient**). This requires a lot of energy.

The Concentration Gradient – "Waiting in Line at Checkout"

Story time! Let's say you run out to buy the latest, best ever phone on the very first day it is released. You get to the store, grab the phone, go to checkout, only to be greeted by a checkout line with twenty people already in it! Bummer. Only, wait! A new line is opening up. Hold on to this moment. You can wait on the line with twenty people ahead of you or you can move into the line with no one in front of you. Do you move? Of course, you do! Do you move quickly? Again, yes. Do other shoppers also move? Yes. When do the shoppers stop moving? The shoppers stop moving when the two lines become about equally long.

When molecules do this, it is referred to as **diffusion**. The difference in concentration (*in this case people in line*) is referred to as the **concentration gradient**. *In our shopping example above, the concentration gradient was high; twenty shoppers in one row and zero shoppers in the other.* In this case the molecules (*shoppers*) move very quickly until **equilibrium** (both sides are about equal) is reached. If the concentration gradient were low (*let's say 12 shoppers in one line and 10 in the other*), movement would be slower until equilibrium was reached.

It is easy to move **with** the concentration gradient. *You will easily move from a line with twenty people to a line with zero waiting, thank you very much! This does not require any energy. However, what if you were asked to move from the line with no waiting to the line with twenty people? You would not like that one bit! That goes against what you want!* In molecules, this goes **against** the concentration gradient. This requires a LOT of energy! The store employee may just have to drag you, kicking and screaming[3], into the line with more people!

- **With** the concentration gradient/**down** the concentration gradient – no energy used – **passive** transport.
- **Against** the concentration gradient/**up** the concentration gradient – lots of energy used – **active** transport.

First Up, Passive Transport

These do NOT require energy.

Diffusion

Okay. You got your phone! Now let's have a party! The quarantine is lifted, and it is safe to have a fantastic big party. You really want it to be great. It's a beautiful early autumn night and you put out the guacamole and throw open the doors to your house. A few people arrive. Very few. You get nervous. You notice that there is a great concentration of some younger kids hanging out on your street (I don't know why). There is a lesser concentration of people in your party. So, you invite them in! The people move from an area of greater concentration (the street) to an area of lesser concentration (your party). They continue to mill in and out, until equilibrium is reached. That is, the amount of people in your party is about the same as the amount of people outside. This requires no energy from the people or you. It happens quite spontaneously.

This is **diffusion**. This is how molecules, such as oxygen and carbon dioxide, come in and out of your cells. They

---

[3] I don't condone kicking or screaming in a store. Or hassling store employees. It's just a visual for how much energy that might take! It's for biology! Do not get in trouble!

move from a higher concentration to a lesser concentration until equilibrium is reached. This is very important because every cell in your body needs a fresh supply of oxygen constantly. This is the very reason we breathe! And while our cells are receiving oxygen, they are releasing carbon dioxide in the same manner.

So, *the party* is the *cell*. And *the people* are oxygen and carbon dioxide.

Osmosis is a form of diffusion. It deals with fluids, most notably water. It does not require energy from the cell. It is passive. It also really confuses many students. I know why it confuses you. For a long time, it confused me too. I have included a side story to clear up the confusion (see Story 5b: Exploding Fish).

Facilitated Diffusion

It's later in the evening and your party is now packed! You decide no one else can come in. A few moments later, the most famous DJ in the land shows up. Your friend, Sam, cannot find you, but decides that the party would be so much better if that DJ was allowed to come in and do her thing. Sam tells her to run around to the back of the house, where there is an open window. She is to jump up to the open window. Sam will then catch her and pull her inside. Now, Sam will not help anyone else get into the party this way – only this particular DJ. And Sam will only help because the party really needs the DJ to keep its energy going!

In this little story, Sam is playing the part of a carrier protein. Carrier proteins are embedded in the cell membrane *(like a window is embedded in a house).* Carrier proteins are shaped to fit a certain type of molecule. This is how glucose enters the cell. Remember that glucose is a carbohydrate and that carbohydrates provide energy for the cell.

Glucose is too large of a molecule to enter the cell through diffusion. So it needs a carrier protein to help it through. This is called facilitated diffusion. It does not require energy from the cell. It is another form of passive transport.

Again, *Sam* is the carrier protein. *Your house/party* is the cell. *The DJ* is glucose.

Ion Channels

There is one thing I forgot to mention about your house and that is that it has a few tunnels.

These are specific to one thing (*one person*). Channels (*tunnels*) can be opened or closed with gates depending on the situation.

Going back to your party, you may have said that no one else can come in. However, there is a tunnel that goes from your best friend's house to yours. Your best friend is welcome to come and go as they please. They are your best friend! You always want them at your house/party/whatever. So, you always leave this tunnel open. You may have another tunnel just for your grandmother. Now, you love your grandmother – but you may not want your dear grandmother at your packed party. You shut that gate. However, the following Sunday afternoon, after the party has ended and Grandma has offered to come by with dinner and pie, you swing that gate wide open.

Remember, it depends on the needs of the cell at any given time what molecules can enter and leave. Ions such as calcium (Ca^{++}) and chloride (Cl-) enter the cell through **ion channels**.

In this example *your house* is the cell, *the tunnels* are ion channels, *your best friend* is calcium, and *your grandmother* is chloride.

Active Transport

These require energy.

Sodium-Potassium Pump

*At this point, your party is the party of all times. It is epic. It is also packed. You declare that no one else is getting in no matter what! And then it happens. The tour bus for your favorite band pulls up outside of your house. And breaks down. It is really hot outside and the band members (including your favorite singer EVER) get off of the bus and are just standing there in your yard! Obviously, they have to come to your party. This would make you a legend! But there is no room at your party. So... remember those younger kids you invited to the party a few hours ago? They need to go. But they do not want to go. You have some rather large, strong friends. They pick up these kids, **three** at a time, and drag them (kicking and screaming[4]) out of your party. These large, strong friends then pick up the band members, **two** at a time, and drag them into your party. The band does not really want to be at your party. This all takes a lot of energy! Also, as soon as your friends deposit the younger kids outside, they try to run right back in. Likewise, as soon as your friends deposit the band on the inside, they try to run right back outside.*

In this part of the story, *your house/party* is the cell. Your *strong friends* are **carrier proteins** (here in active transport, they are called **pumps**). The *younger kids* are **sodium (Na⁺)** and the *band members* are **potassium (K⁺)**. There are other types of pumps in living things, but this sodium-potassium pump is the one that is talked about

---

[4] Once again, you should not drag people against their will anywhere! This is a story to help you remember the sodium-potassium pump. This is not reality.

most often. This type of transport carries 3 positive charges (*younger children*) out for every 2 positive charges (*band members*) that it brings in. The difference in the charges across the cell membrane is what enables nerves to conduct signals to and from your brain.

Endocytosis

Another form of active transport **into** a cell is endocytosis. "Endo" means **in**side, "cyto" means cell.

At this point a friend walks up your driveway and wants to come into your party. There are more people inside your party than outside, so your late-coming friend cannot come in through diffusion. Your friend is not water, so osmosis is not possible. Your friend is not the cool DJ, so facilitated diffusion is not available for him. Your friend is not your best friend or your grandmother so ion channels are not an option. Your friend is also not a member of your favorite band, so he cannot enter your house through the sodium-potassium pump.

There is another way. But it uses a lot of energy.

Your friend stands very close to the outside wall of your house. The partygoers inside assemble more of the bricks and mortar that your house is made from and they begin to build an extension of your house around your late-coming friend. Once that extension is built, they dissolve the original wall and, "presto," your late-coming friend is now in the cell … party! I mean party! Endocytosis!

- If the molecule being brought into the cell is a fluid, this is called **pinocytosis** (cell drinking).
- If the molecule being brought into the cell is a whole cell or solid, this is called **phagocytosis** (cell eating). This is how some of our white blood cells engulf and destroy some bacteria. This is also how some single-celled organisms (like amoeba) eat.

41

Exocytosis

The process of exocytosis is the opposite of endocytosis, and it is an energy-demanding process for getting things **out** of the cell. "Exo" means **out**. "Cyto" means cell.

It is time for a certain partygoer to leave. That person is chasing people around with guacamole on their fingers and is generally being a nuisance. You and your fellow partygoers form a dance circle around them and start moving the circle over to the wall on the inside of the house. Then you quickly install a large sliding door next to the guacamole kid, open it, and slide him out. Exocytosis!

This is how the cell gets rid of large waste material. It is also how some larger proteins are packaged to leave the cell. A **vesicle** (just a temporary storage pouch) forms around the particle. The vesicle then fuses to the cell membrane. The molecules that make up the cell membrane rearrange themselves. The proteins and lipids that make up the cell membrane are constantly moving and rearranging themselves anyway (**fluid mosaic model**). The cell membrane opens to the outside of the cell and... the particle is out.

Sciency Words

Selectively permeable – a property of cellular membranes that only allows certain molecules to enter or exit the cell.

Concentration gradient – results from the unequal distribution of particles, e.g. ions, between two solutions (for example between the inside and outside of a cell).

Diffusion – the net movement of anything from a region of higher concentration to a region of lower concentration.

Equilibrium – a state of balance or a stable situation where opposing forces cancel each other out and where no changes are occurring.

Osmosis – the movement of water through a semipermeable membrane according to the concentration gradient of water across the membrane.

Carrier protein – proteins that carry substances from one side of a biological membrane to the other.

Facilitated diffusion – the passive movement of molecules across the cell membrane via the aid of a membrane protein.

Glucose – the simple sugar that is the chief source of energy. Glucose is found in the blood and is the main sugar that the body manufactures.

Ion channel – protein expressed by virtually all living cells that creates a pathway for charged ions from dissolved salts (including sodium, potassium, calcium, and chloride ions) to pass through the otherwise impermeant lipid cell membrane.

Sodium-potassium pump – enzyme-based mechanism that maintains correct cellular concentrations of **sodium** and **potassium** ions by removing excess ions from inside a cell and replacing them with ions from outside the cell.

Phagocytosis – or "cell eating," is the process by which a cell engulfs a particle and digests it.

Pinocytosis – or "cell drinking," the ingestion of liquid into a cell by the budding of small vesicles from the cell membrane.

Vesicle – small structures within a cell, consisting of fluid enclosed by a lipid bilayer. They are involved in transport, buoyancy control, and enzyme storage.

Fluid mosaic model – describes the structure of cell membranes. In this model, a flexible layer made of lipid molecules is interspersed with large protein molecules that function as channels through which other molecules enter and leave the cell.

STORY 5B: EXPLODING FISH (OSMOSIS)[5]

A Side Story About Osmosis

Osmosis is the diffusion of water across a semipermeable membrane. When water flows across a cell membrane, without the use of energy from the cell, that is osmosis. Osmosis is a form of diffusion. It is that easy.

And yet, many students miss osmosis questions on tests and get confused in their thinking. It often seems to be the opposite of diffusion. It is not. Osmosis is the way that **WATER** will move. Osmosis is when the **molecules** (salts, sugars, etc.) **cannot** pass through the membrane, but the **water can**. Remember when we talked about **homeostasis**? The definition of homeostasis is the ability or tendency to maintain internal stability in an organism to compensate for environmental changes. An example of homeostasis is the human body keeping an average temperature of 98.6 degrees F.

In the case of osmosis, it is the water that is moving to maintain homeostasis. If your blood contains a lot of salt and your cells have very little salt, the water will flow from your cells into your blood. If you eat a lot of salty chips, the salt level in your blood rises. Water flows from your cells into your blood to try and maintain homeostasis (keep the salt level the same throughout your body). When your cells lose that water, they signal your brain that they need water and you feel thirsty (and hopefully drink some water).

---

[5] No fish were ever harmed in the telling of this story. Fish should not be harmed for stories.

Now, about those fish. Saltwater fish, like tuna, live in a very salty environment. Their bodies contain more fresh-water, water with less salt than the ocean around them. The salt in the ocean cannot pass directly through their cell membranes, but water can. The freshwater from a tuna's cells is constantly **leaving** the tuna in an attempt to make the water in the ocean the same concentration as the water in the tuna. Tuna, and other saltwater fish, must **drink** a lot of water or they would constantly dehydrate. (Saltwater fish have a special gland to deal with the excess salt that they drink. They can drink saltwater without any adverse health effects. Most animals, including humans, do not have this gland and should not normally drink salt water).

Freshwater fish have the opposite problem. The cells in their bodies contain more salt than the surrounding fresh-water. The salt should diffuse from the higher concentration in the fish's cells to the lower concentration in the surrounding water. However, the *salt cannot diffuse because it is too large to get through the membrane.* Therefore the water will move, in an attempt to restore homeostasis. In freshwater fish, the water moves from the lake (freshwater) **into** the fish's cells. The fish needs to constantly **urinate** in order to expel all the excess water.

Picture yourself swimming in a nice, cool lake on a hot sum-mer day. Picture all the hundreds (or thousands) of fish peeing all around you. That is a wonderful picture! It will help you remember osmosis! Also, if freshwater organisms didn't constantly expel excess water, their cells would ex-plode! Nothing would break the calm of that lovely cool swim through the lake like hundreds of exploding fish!

Sciency Words

Homeostasis – the tendency toward a relatively stable equilibrium between interdependent elements, especially as maintained by physiological processes.

Osmosis – the movement of **water** through a membrane to try to make the concentrations of the fluid the same on both sides.

STORY #6: THE TRUE STORY OF THE CARROT (PHOTOSYNTHESIS PART 1)

Photosynthesis

Consider this story of a carrot plant. It is spring and you plant a carrot seed in the ground. You water it and, soon, two little leaves shoot up from the ground. The leaves turn ever so slightly toward the sun and it begins. "Photosynthesis, photosynthesis," you can hear in the gentle breeze. The carrot grows and many more leaves develop. Even more photosynthesis! That little carrot plant works very hard all throughout the spring. The summer brings even more growth and development. Day in and day out, those leaves collect sunlight. The roots of the plant shoot further in the soil and absorb water and minerals. While you are out enjoying summer with family and friends, the little carrot plant works very hard. It has an important task. It. Is. Making. A. Carrot.

Did you ever consider why a carrot plant makes a carrot? (Yes, I do assume you are a rational being who thinks rational thoughts so why the heck would you ever ponder such a thing?) Seriously though, why does a carrot plant make a carrot? When I first thought about it, I thought it was so we could have something colorful, nutritious, and crunchy in our salads. I was thinking about myself and how a carrot benefits me. How self-centered I was being!

A carrot plant does not care about me. It doesn't care about you either. A carrot plant, like much of life, only wants to do one thing. Survive. So why does a carrot plant make a carrot? Most of the time my students cannot answer that question. It is a foreign thought for us. The reason a carrot plant makes a carrot all spring and summer long is the same reason a squirrel puts away corn and nuts all season long. Survival. The squirrel is squirreling away (pun intended!) food so that it has something to eat in the winter.

The carrot plant is storing up food (the carrot!) so that it has something to eat in the winter!

Of course, we do not allow this to happen. We wait until autumn. Oh yes, late in the autumn, after the carrot plant has worked as hard as it possibly could to make that crisp, orange, nutritious carrot – we kill the carrot plant, steal its beautiful carrot, and use all the nutrients for ourselves. And then we have a harvest festival.

That is the true story of a carrot.

****

What if this story had a different ending? What if, upon hearing this story, you decide to save the carrot? You build a little greenhouse, or move somewhere warm. You protect the plant from insects and deer. All winter long you water the plant and you let that carrot plant live. Finally, in the early spring, some family member comes along and picks that carrot. What has happened to the firm, orange, crisp carrot? That carrot would now be wilted, smaller, and almost depleted. That's because the plant would have used the nutrients stored in the carrot to keep itself fed and alive during the winter.

That is why a carrot plant makes a carrot.

This story has many points when it comes to understanding biology. Actually, it is integral to so much science. We tend to think in terms of how life and nature serve us – that is, how other life forms and nature serve humans. Other life does not live to serve us. It has its own agenda.

The Point of the Traumatic Carrot Story #1:

Law of Energy:

- Energy cannot be created or destroyed. It only changes form.
- All energy comes from the sun. That is important, so I'll repeat. All energy comes from the sun.

In our story, **radiant energy** came from the sun and hit the leaves of the carrot plant. The **chloroplasts** in the plant cells changed that radiant energy into **chemical energy**. The carrot used that chemical energy to live. It used chemical energy to grow, to produce roots, to absorb water, and to make flowers for reproduction. (Yes, carrots reproduce sexually, but I think I've scared you enough for one day, so let's just leave that there for now.) Any remaining chemical energy was stored as – you guessed it – a *carrot*.

When we eat a carrot, we break it down in our digestive systems until it is a simple sugar (monosaccharide, like glucose). Glucose is chemical energy. The glucose exits our digestive system cells (through facilitated diffusion) and enters our bloodstream. The blood (containing the glucose) travels to other cells in our body. Let's say this blood traveled past some muscle cells. The muscle cells take in the glucose (again through facilitated diffusion). The glucose travels through the **cytoplasm** and into the mitochondria of that muscle cell. Muscle cells have LOTS of mitochondria because they need LOTS of energy (ATP – adenosine triphosphate! Will you just memorize that already?!). The mitochondria act as a bonfire and converts the glucose (chemical energy) into ATP (still chemical energy). The ATP (still chemical energy) is then converted into movement (kinetic energy), heat (thermal energy), and fat (stored chemical energy). This is how we can run (kinetic energy), maintain our body temperatures (thermal energy), and build up energy reserves (fat).

Humans and other animals need to eat carrots and other food because we cannot stand in sunlight and convert radiant energy (sunlight) into chemical energy (food). We simply cannot.

- We are **heterotrophs**. A heterotroph is an organism that cannot manufacture its own food by **carbon fixation** and therefore derives its intake of nutrition from other sources of organic carbon, mainly plant or animal matter.
- Most plants (like the carrot) are **autotrophs**. An organism capable of synthesizing its own food from inorganic substances using light or chemical energy. Green plants, algae, and certain bacteria are **autotrophs**.

The Point of the Traumatic Carrot Story #2:

Photosynthesis is the Secret of Life!

If the process of photosynthesis did not exist, we would not exist. Photosynthesis is the moment that life is able to use the incoming solar radiation (radiant energy) and change it into the food we eat. Even if you do not like to eat plants, you most certainly eat something that does rely on plants. Without this process, life would cease to exist[6].

---

[6] It is important to note that many of the earliest forms of life, prokaryotes Archaea and Bacteria, perform **chemosynthesis** not **photosynthesis.** That is, they take chemicals (like sulfur) and carbon dioxide (CO_2) to make glucose instead of using sunlight and carbon dioxide to make glucose. We will talk more about this in the Origin of Life Story

Photosynthesis is the Secret of Life!! We should really have one of those awe inspired moments here! Cue the harp player!

However, in trying to learn more about photosynthesis, scientists discovered it is a **biochemical pathway**. It is complicated. It contains a few energy-carrying compounds that sound and look a bit scary when you are first learning about them. It is easy to get lost in the details. If you find yourself wondering why it is important to learn all the details about photosynthesis, go back and read the last two paragraphs. That is the point of photosynthesis.

The Point of the Traumatic Carrot Story #3

True story. I once received an email from a former student who was in college, taking a biology class. The subject line of the email was "Photosynthesis." The whole body of the email was:

AAAAARRRGGGGHHHHHAAAAARRRRGG
GGHHHHHAAAAARRRGGGGHHHHHAAAA
ARRRRGGGGHHHHHAAAAARRRRGGGGHH
HHHAAAAARRRRGGGGHHHHHAAAAARRR
RGGGGHHHHHAAAAARRRRGGGGHHHHHA
AAAARRRRGGGGHHHHHAAAAARRRRGGG
GHHHHHAAAAARRRRGGGGHHHHHAAAAA
RRRRGGGGHHHHHAAAAARRRRGGGGHHH
HHAAAAARRRRGGGGHHHHHAAAAARRRR
GGGGHHHHH!!

Some students find photosynthesis challenging. Let's break it down into a few sections:

1. Inside a plant cell – p. 41
2. Light Absorption (Our Star Football Player) – p. 43

1. Inside a Plant Cell

Where does photosynthesis take place? In plants. Good. Where in plants? Most photosynthesis takes place in the leaves. Okay, but where in the leaves? Leaves are made up of plant cells and in those plant cells are **chloroplasts**. That is where photosynthesis takes place. Great! Where in chloroplasts does photosynthesis take place? Take a look at the chloroplast diagram below. There can be hundreds of chloroplasts in each plant cell.

Each chloroplast has an outer membrane and an inner membrane. Inside the chloroplasts are thin, flat disks called **thylakoids**. These disks are stacked up on top of one another. Each stack is called a **granum** (plural: grana). Surrounding all of these grana is a sticky liquid called **stroma**.

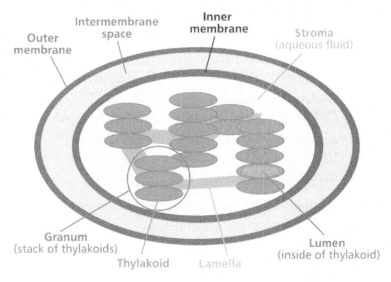

I like to think of the thylakoids as pancakes. No one likes to eat just one pancake. We want a stack of pancakes (like a granum). And no stack of pancakes is complete without syrup – a sticky liquid that covers them! Just like stroma is a sticky liquid that covers the granum!

There is a biology vocabulary issue here. Plants contain both **stoma** and **stroma**:

- **Stoma** (plural: **stomata**) is a small opening in the leaf of a plant that allows carbon dioxide in and oxygen and water vapor out.
- **Stroma**, as noted above, is the sticky liquid that surrounds the grana inside a chloroplast. Both are important in photosynthesis.

I note that stroma has the letter "R" in it and so does the word "syrup." Stoma does not have the letter "R" in it. "R" = "syrup." That will help you differentiate the two vocabulary words.

2. Light Absorption (Our Star Football Player)

There are many **pigments** (compounds that absorb light) involved in photosynthesis. The main one is **chlorophyll a**.

There are other pigments called **accessory pigments**. These include: **Chlorophyll b** and **Carotenoids**[7].

---

[7] If "carotenoids" remind you of carrots, that is good. Some carotenoids reflect orange wavelengths of light.

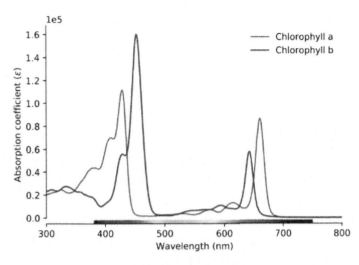

Remember that all radiant energy comes from the sun. The sun's visible spectrum is arranged from largest to smallest wavelengths; red, orange, yellow, green, blue, and violet (ROY G BV). *There is a debate over Sir Isaac Newton including indigo among the wavelengths – most physicists do not include indigo. (These physicists are the same scientists who demoted Pluto, the sphere formerly known as a planet. Which, ironically, appears indigo.)*

Anyhow... Chlorophyll a, as you can see from the chart above, **absorbs** light energy in the violet, blue and red ranges. Chlorophyll a **reflects** light in the green ranges. This is why most plant leaves appear green.

You will notice that chlorophyll b also **absorbs** light in the blue and red ranges, but at slightly different wavelengths. Chlorophyll b also **reflects** light in the green wavelength ranges.

The carotenoids absorb light in still other wavelength ranges. They may **reflect** light in the red, yellow, or orange ranges.

In the fall, when daylight is decreasing, many plants stop manufacturing chlorophyll a and b in anticipation of the winter. As the chlorophyll is no longer being produced, it is easier for us to see the reflected light coming off of the carotenoids. That is why leaves that had appeared green all season long now appear yellow, red, or orange.

I describe chlorophyll a as the star football player. When the team has a truly remarkable athlete, it is fun to watch them play. It is fun to watch that outstanding athlete block five opponents at once, while our team scores and wins, time after time. If you are a sports fan, you may spend the rest of the week talking about all the wonderful plays that you saw on the field. You can't wait to see what that player will do next week and you show up at the game with your eyes on our star player.

Football is a team sport. There are other players on the team. Even the best player can't block ALL of the opponents while being the quarterback, receiver, and kicker! The team has other blockers, the quarterback is there, and so is the kicker. They are all doing their job every single week, all season long! We just don't see them. Star play #1 is outshining them all. That player gets all the news coverage. That player gets all the glory.

Perhaps star player #1 gets the flu and needs to sit out a game. We are still fans. We want to cheer for someone. All of a sudden, you may find yourself asking, "Who else is on the team?" You may find yourself appreciating the other players and begin cheering for them. The other players, rightfully, think, "Wait a minute. We have been here all season long! We are doing a good job! Why is it only now that the fans are noticing us?"

That is like chlorophyll a. It outshines (or out-**reflects**) the other pigments. It is only when the chlorophyll pigments stop being produced in the fall that we are able to see the wavelengths of light (red, orange, yellow) that are being reflected by the carotenoids and other accessory pigments. That is why leaves appear many different colors in the fall! The leaves don't really *change* colors. Chlorophyll a just goes away and we are able to *see* the other colors that were there all along.

3. Electron Transport Chains & Chemiosmosis (the Light Reactions)

The processes described in this chapter are called the **Light Reactions** because they require light energy. Sunlight is used to start both Photosystem II and Photosystem I by "energizing" an electron.

As we talked about earlier, thylakoids are the thin, pancake-like disks inside the chloroplast. Thylakoids are made up of chlorophyll pigment molecules. They have a lipid bilayer, just like the cell. Accessory pigments can also be embedded in the thylakoid. There are two known **photosystems** that take place here. They are **Photosystem I** and **Photosystem II** – because sometimes science makes sense. Photosystem II happens first – because sometimes science does not make sense. (Photosystem I was discovered first.) However, Photosystem II must happen first, so that is where we will start.

Photosystem II

Here is the overall equation for photosynthesis.

Sunlight + $6CO_2$ + $12H_2O$ → $C_6H_{12}O_6$ + $6O_2$ + $6H_2O$

            (Carbon   (Water)   (Glucose)   (Oxygen)   (Water)
            dioxide)

At the start of Photosystem II, so much radiant energy (sunlight) is being absorbed by a chlorophyll molecule that it gets an "excited" electron. That electron "jumps" to a higher energy level. Because the original chlorophyll molecule has lost an electron, it obtains a positive (+) charge. It will need that electron to be replaced in order to function again.

Meanwhile, the "excited" electron needs somewhere to go, so it attaches to a nearby chlorophyll molecule. This nearby electron acceptor is called the **primary electron acceptor**. This electron then gets bounced around to a series of chlorophyll molecules through what we call the **electron transport chain** of **Photosystem II**. As the electron is getting passed along this chain of molecules, it is losing energy. That energy is being stored as positive (+) charges inside the thylakoid.

At home, if you are wearing socks, you may drag your feet along the carpet in order to build up an electrical charge. You want to use this charge to "shock" your little brother. Just like that, the electron is dragging itself over chlorophyll molecules to build up a charge to be used later.

After the electron is done going through the electron transport chain of Photosystem II, the last molecule (very temporarily) holds that electron.

Photosystem I

Meanwhile, radiant energy (sunlight) is also being absorbed by a chlorophyll molecule in Photosystem I. Like before, so much solar radiation is absorbed that the molecule gets an "excited" electron. This electron jumps to a higher energy level and needs somewhere to be accepted. The electron is accepted by the **primary electron acceptor** of Photosystem I. This new electron jumps around to another series of chlorophyll molecules known as the **electron transport chain** of **Photosystem I.**

Once again, as the electron jumps from molecule to molecule, it loses energy and charge is built up inside the thylakoid.

In order to restore the electron lost at the start of Photosystem I, the electron left at the end of Photosystem II is given to the start of Photosystem I. We say that Photosystem II *restores* Photosystem I.

We now have an "extra" electron at the end of Photosystem I. This electron combines with a proton and **NADP⁺** to create **NADPH.** NADPH is one of the end products of the light reactions of photosynthesis. We definitely want NADPH.

Stick with me here. If you are like my students, this is the part where you feel overwhelmed and want to give up. Don't. Three more little things and we'll call it a day. Take a break if you need to, but don't give up!

We are at a point where we are going to have to deal with some energy-carrying molecules. NADPH is an energy-carrying molecule.

NADPH is like a gift card to your favorite coffee shop, which has $20 on it. It has energy behind it and that energy can be used to do things, like buy coffee. NADP⁺ *is like that same gift card when it doesn't have any money left. It can't be used to do anything (no coffee for you). However, if you were to charge that card up again and put another $20 on it, it would now have energy behind it again!*

- NADPH = charged-up gift card ($$)
- NADP⁺ = empty gift card

You can think of Photosystem I and Photosystem II as putting the energy ($$) back onto the empty gift card.

Restoring Photosystem II

Remember when the first chlorophyll molecule of Photosystem II was left with a missing electron? In order for the photosystems to be ready for another round of **electron transport**, that electron must be replaced. The replacement of that electron comes from the splitting of two water molecules.

$$2H_2O > 4H^+ + 4e + O_2$$

For every **2** water molecules that split (by the action of a water splitting enzyme), **4** electrons are obtained. One of those electrons is used to *restore* Photosystem II. So, for every **2** water molecules split, Photosystem II can be restored **4** times.

This is the reason we need to water our plants and gardens. To restore Photosystem II.

The protons produced ($4H^+$) help to build up the charge in the thylakoid. The oxygen is given off as a waste product.

Do you mean to tell me that humans and other animals evolved to live off the WASTE PRODUCTS of plants?! Yes. Yes, we did.

The final step of the light reactions is called **chemiosmosis**.

Chemiosmosis

- There is a protein embedded in the thylakoid membrane known as **ATP synthase.** ATP synthase is a carrier protein that allows the positive charge (protons H^+) that was built up in the thylakoid to cross the thylakoid membrane. As the protons cross the thylakoid membrane, their energy is used to combine **ADP** (adenosine diphosphate) with another phosphate, creating **ATP** (adenosine triphosphate).

- ADP^+ + phosphate > ATP
  - ADP^+ = empty gift card
  - ATP = charged-up gift card ($$)

ATP is the second energy-carrying product of the light re-actions of photosynthesis.

The End Products of the Light Reactions

The two energy-carrying end products (*charged-up gift cards*) of the light reactions of photosynthesis are:

- **NADPH**
- **ATP**

Now that we have our charged-up gift cards, we can make **glucose**. That happens in the next chapter, during the Calvin Cycle.

Sciency Words

Radiant energy – The energy from the sun is called radi-ant energy, or *energy possessed by vibrating particles*.

Chloroplasts – a cell organelle that produces energy through photosynthesis.

Chemical energy – the energy which is stored in the bonds of chemical compounds (molecules and atoms). It is released in certain chemical reactions, and mostly pro-duces heat as a by-product (then known as an exothermic reaction). Examples of stored chemical energy are bio-mass, batteries, natural gas, petroleum, and coal.

Cytoplasm – The jellylike material that makes up much of a cell inside the cell membrane. In eukaryotic cells, the cy-toplasm surrounds the nucleus.

Heterotroph – An organism that cannot synthesize its own food and is dependent upon complex organic substances for nutrition.

Autotroph – An organism capable of synthesizing its own food from inorganic substances using light or chemical energy.

Biochemical pathway – the long chains of chemical reactions that take place in the normal operation of living systems.

Chemosynthesis – a process in which some organisms use chemical energy instead of light energy to produce "food."

Photosynthesis – a process used by plants and other organisms to convert light energy into chemical energy that can later be released to fuel the organisms' activities.

Thylakoid – membrane-bound compartments inside chloroplasts and cyanobacteria. They are the site of the light-dependent reactions of photosynthesis.

Granum (plural: **grana**) – the collective term for the stack of thylakoids within the chloroplast of plant cells.

Stroma – the colorless fluid surrounding the grana within the chloroplast.

Stoma – a tiny pore in the surface of a leaf that is used for gas exchange.

Pigments – substances produced by living organisms that have a color resulting from selective color absorption.

Chlorophyll a – a specific form of chlorophyll used in photosynthesis. It absorbs most energy from wavelengths of violet–blue and orange–red light. It also reflects green–yellow light, and as such contributes to the observed green color of most plants.

Chlorophyll b – helps in photosynthesis by absorbing light energy.

Accessory pigments – light-absorbing compounds, found in photosynthetic organisms, which work in conjunction with chlorophyll a.

Carotenoids – a type of accessory pigment, created by plants to help them absorb light energy and convert it to chemical energy.

Photosystems – functional and structural units of protein complexes involved in photosynthesis. Together, they carry out the primary photochemistry of photosynthesis: the absorption of light and the transfer of energy and electrons. Photosystems are found in the thylakoid membranes of plants, algae, and cyanobacteria.

Photosystem I – an integral membrane protein complex that uses light energy to catalyze the transfer of electrons across the thylakoid membrane. Ultimately, the electrons that are transferred by Photosystem I are used to produce the high-energy carrier NADPH.

Photosystem II – The photosystem that absorbs light for oxidation of water.

Primary electron acceptor – A specialized molecule sharing the reaction center with the pair of reaction-center chlorophyll a molecules; it accepts an electron from one of these two chlorophylls.

Electron transport chain – a series of molecules that accept or donate electrons easily. By moving step-by-step through these, electrons are moved in a specific direction across a membrane. The movement of hydrogen ions are coupled with this. This means that when electrons are moved, hydrogen ions move too.

Chemiosmosis – the movement of ions across a semiper-meable membrane-bound structure, down their electrochemical gradient. An example of this would be the formation of adenosine triphosphate (ATP) by the movement of hydrogen ions (H^+) across a membrane during cellular respiration or photosynthesis.

ATP synthase – An enzyme that catalyzes the formation of ATP from the phosphorylation of ADP with inorganic phosphate, using a form of energy such as the energy from a proton gradient.

STORY #7: CAN WE GET SOME FOOD? (THE CALVIN CYCLE; PHOTOSYNTHESIS PART 2)

The Calvin Cycle – Still Photosynthesis

The Calvin Cycle is the final step in photosynthesis. The Calvin Cycle is also known as

1. The dark reactions
2. The light-independent reactions

These reactions do not *require* light energy. They were discovered by a man named Melvin Calvin. That is a fun name to say. Here is the overall formula for photosynthesis, once again:

$$\text{Sunlight} + 6CO_2 + 12H_2O \rightarrow C_6H_{12}O_6 + 6O_2 + 6H_2O$$

| (Carbon dioxide) | (Water) | (Glucose) | (Oxygen) | (Water) |

Let's look at each part of this formula. Think back to Story #6 and the light reactions – Photosystems II and I and chemiosmosis.

- Did we discuss sunlight? Yes. Yes, we did. Sunlight is used to start both Photosystem II and Photosystem I by "energizing" an electron.
- Did we discuss carbon dioxide (CO_2)? No.
- Did we discuss water (H_2O)? Yes. You will recall that two water molecules were split to supply the electrons that restore Photosystem II. That reaction also supplies protons and oxygen gas. Oxygen gas is released as a waste product (although it is very important to the animal kingdom).

- Did we produce any glucose during the light reactions? Nope.
- Did we produce oxygen (O_2)? Yes – from the splitting of water that we just mentioned.

Besides oxygen (O_2), what did we get out of the light reactions? We got 2 different energy carriers: NADPH and ATP **(our charged-up gift** cards ($$)).

From NADPH, ATP, and Carbon Dioxide to Glucose

The Calvin Cycle takes NADPH and ATP and carbon dioxide (CO_2) and produces Glucose ($C_6H_{12}O_6$).

The Calvin Cycle takes place in the stroma of the chloroplast. (Remember the R: stroma – it is like syrup!) Carbon dioxide (one carbon) diffuses into the stroma and combines with a 5-carbon compound (RuBP). This forms a 6-carbon compound which immediately splits into 2 3-carbon compounds (PGA).

Now we use our gift cards!

2 molecules of ATP are used. They are converted back into 2 ADPs and 2 phosphates. Also, 2 molecules of NADPH are used. They are converted back to 2 molecules of NADP$^+$.

These "empty gift cards" (ADP and NADP$^+$) now go back to the thylakoid membrane to be "charged up" again by the light reactions.)

In using the energy stored in ATP and NADPH, the molecules PGA were converted to 2 molecules of PGAL.

This is like using an oven to bake a cake. The ingredients in the batter are the same as the ingredients in the cake. However, the energy in the oven causes a chemical reaction which makes a baked cake a very different thing from the batter. PGAL is a very different thing from PGA. The energy in ATP and NADPH has caused a chemical change.

Each of the two molecules of PGAL had 3 carbons. So, together they add up to 6 carbons in total. 5 of those carbons are converted back to RuBP and the cycle can start over again. It does require the energy in 1 more molecule of ATP to make this change. What happens to the remaining carbon? It makes glucose! Glucose ($C_6H_{12}O_6$) is a 6-carbon compound. Therefore, it takes 6 turns of the Calvin Cycle to make 1 molecule of glucose.

However, it is not always glucose that is produced: These are plants! They produce carrots, strawberries, celery, lettuce, and peanuts! These compounds (foods!) DO contain glucose. They can also contain other carbohydrates (like fructose and starch), proteins, and lipids. But remember, all those things are carbon-based. Turn the Calvin Cycle wheel and get a peanut, a grape, some wheat! Photosynthesis is the secret to life! Cue the harp player!

Sciency Words

NADPH – stands for nicotinamide adenine dinucleotide phosphate hydrogen. … NADPH is a product of the first stage of photosynthesis and is used to help fuel the reactions that take place in the second stage of photosynthesis.

ATP (adenosine triphosphate) – energy-carrying molecule found in the cells of all living things.

Story #8: Now That We Found Food, What Are We Gonna Do with It? (Cellular Respiration)

Cellular Respiration

One biochemical pathway down (photosynthesis).

One biochemical pathway to go (cellular respiration).

In photosynthesis, we explore how sunlight (energy) is turned into food.

In cellular respiration, we explore how food is turned back into energy.

All living things need energy to move, grow, reproduce, and heat their bodies. All living things must be able to perform cellular respiration. If you look at the formulas for photosynthesis and cellular respiration, you will see that they are basically opposite of each other. One turns an energy source (sunlight) into food (glucose) and the other turns food (glucose) into an energy source (ATP).

Photosynthesis:

Sunlight + $6CO_2$ + $12H_2O$ > $C_6H_{12}O_6$ + $6O_2$

(Carbon dioxide) (Water) (Glucose) (Oxygen)

Cellular Respiration:

$C_6H_{12}O_6$ + $6O_2$ > $6CO_2$ + $6H_2O$ + ATP

(Glucose) (Oxygen) (Carbon dioxide) (Water) (Adenosine Triphosphate)

The first step of cellular respiration is **glycolysis**. Glycolysis takes place in the cytoplasm of the cell. Glycolysis takes 6-carbon glucose and, through a series of chemical reactions, gives us 2 3-carbon molecules of **pyruvic acid**.

This reaction uses 2 ATP molecules (*gift cards!*) at the start. However, at the end of the reaction, 4 ATP molecules are released. So, there is a net gain of 2 ATP molecules produced for every molecule of glucose that is broken down into pyruvic acid.

Also used in this reaction is another energy-carrying compound (*gift card!*). This one is called NAD^+. Two NAD^+ are converted to NADPH for every molecule of glucose converted to pyruvic acid.

- NADH = fully charged gift card ($$)
- NAD+ = empty gift card

Story time! Let's say that the only way you can make money is to go to biology class every day. It costs you $2 to drive to biology class. You also need 2 empty gift cards (*NAD^+). I'll explain how you get those in a minute. At the end of class, you receive $4 and 2 fully charged gift cards.*

Now that is not very much money. However, you do make a profit of $2 – it is a very small profit but it might be enough to keep you going. Before you can make money the next day by going to biology class again, you need to:

1. Save $2 for driving to class the next day.
2. Empty those 2 gift cards.

The money is molecules of ATP. *Biology class* is the process of glycolysis.

What do we get out of glycolysis? We get 2 molecules (net) of ATP. We get 2 molecules of NADH and H^+. We get 2 molecules of pyruvic acid.

ATP is energy needed for life. NADH and H⁺ are energy carriers (gift cards). Pyruvic acid is an acid. What do we do with pyruvic acid?

What Happens to Pyruvic Acid?

IT DEPENDS!

(Students like that answer...)

What does it depend on? Oxygen!

- If there is NO oxygen in the cell > **anaerobic** pathways
- If there IS oxygen in the cell > **aerobic** pathway

Anaerobic Pathways

Let's discuss the anaerobic pathways first. **Anaerobic** processes are processes that can happen *without* oxygen. There are many anaerobic pathways that have been identified in biology. We will talk about the two most commonly mentioned pathways: **Lactic acid fermentation** and **Alcoholic Fermentation**.

Lactic Acid Fermentation

In lactic acid fermentation, 3-carbon pyruvic acid is converted (chemically) to 3-carbon lactic acid. This chemical reaction takes NADH and H⁺ and converts it to NAD⁺. This (empty *gift card*) NAD⁺ is now able to go back to glycolysis and keep the glycolysis going. And since glycolysis gave us 2 molecules of pyruvic acid, 2 NAD⁺ can now be regenerated.

The microorganisms that perform lactic acid fermentation give off the lactic acid as a waste product. **For the microorganisms, the process is all about regenerating NAD⁺ so**

73

that they can keep glycolysis going. Remember, glycolysis does not generate much ATP (2 molecules), but that is enough to keep some microorganisms going. However, the lactic acid that is produced by these microorganisms is used in the production of cheese and yogurt, so that is good for us.

Your muscle cells can also go through lactic acid fermentation if they run out of oxygen. Normally, muscle cells store oxygen and go through aerobic respiration. However, if you are working those muscles especially hard, they may run out of oxygen and temporarily switch over to anaerobic respiration. This causes your muscle cells to produce very little energy (ATP) and lots of lactic acid. Lactic acid makes your muscles feel sore and painful. When you are athletically training, you are "training" your muscle cells to hold more oxygen so that, over time, you won't feel as sore the next day. And you'll have more energy if your cells stay aerobic.

Alcoholic Fermentation

In alcoholic fermentation, 3-carbon pyruvic acid is converted (chemically) to 2-carbon ethyl alcohol (ethanol). This chemical reaction takes NADH and H^+ and converts it to NAD^+. This (empty *gift card*) NAD^+ is now able to go back to glycolysis and **keep the glycolysis going.** And since glycolysis gave us 2 molecules of pyruvic acid, 2 NAD^+ can be regenerated.

Ethyl alcohol is a waste product for the microorganisms that use this pathway. Alcoholic fermentation also gives us 1-carbon carbon dioxide (CO_2). This is also given off as a waste product for the organisms that use this pathway. Humans put the ethyl alcohol to use to make beer, wine, and bread. The "bubbles" that the carbon dioxide creates is used to make the bread dough rise and to put the "sparkle" in sparkling champagne!

The maximum efficiency for anaerobic respiration is 3.5%.

Aerobic Pathway

This is what most animal cells do.

Let's review: a molecule of glucose enters the cell and is now in the cell's cytoplasm. There it goes through glycolysis. Glycolysis yields a very little bit of ATP (2 molecules) and 2 pyruvic acid molecules. What happens to the pyruvic acid? It depends! What does it depend on? It depends on whether there is oxygen in the cell or not. No oxygen? Anaerobic pathways (mentioned above). Oxygen? Well, if there *is* oxygen present in the cell, the pyruvic acid will diffuse into the **mitochondria** and aerobic respiration will begin.

As the pyruvic acid diffuses through the mitochondrial membrane, 3-carbon pyruvic acid changes to 2-carbon acetyl CoA. The extra carbon is released as CO_2.

The 2-carbon acetyl CoA then goes through 2 processes:

1. Krebs Cycle (Citric Acid Cycle)
2. Electron Transport Chain of Cellular Respiration

These processes will generate a total of up to 38 ATP molecules for every glucose molecule that enters the cell!

The maximum efficiency of aerobic cellular respiration is 66%.

This is enough to keep large, multicellular animals (like humans) energized and ready to go!

Sciency Words

Aerobic – with oxygen.

Anaerobic – without oxygen.

Pyruvic Acid – is an organic acid that probably occurs in all living cells. It ionizes to give a hydrogen ion and an anion, termed pyruvate. Biochemists use the terms *pyruvate* and *pyruvic acid* almost interchangeably.

Glycolysis – Glycolysis is the metabolic pathway that converts glucose ($C_6H_{12}O_6$) into pyruvate (CH_3COCOO^-), and a hydrogen ion (H?). The free energy released in this process is used to form the high-energy molecules ATP and NADH. Glycolysis is a sequence of ten enzyme-catalyzed reactions.

Mitochondria – membrane-bound organelle found in the cytoplasm of almost all eukaryotic cells. Its primary function is to generate large quantities of energy in the form of adenosine triphosphate (ATP).

Story #9: The Book of You (Karyotypes and DNA)

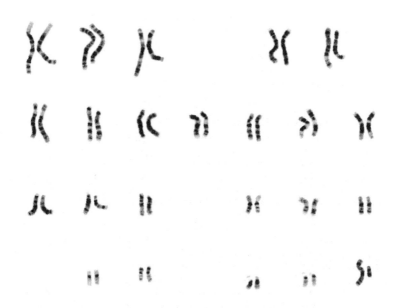

There it is. The book of you. This picture is called a **karyotype.**

When your cells are dividing, the **nuclear membrane** dissolves. Now your DNA is just floating around willy-nilly in the cytoplasm. That does not last for long because the DNA starts to wind itself up around a protein. This is what creates **chromosomes**, like the ones seen above.

Perhaps you have a string on the hood of your sweatshirt. You are playing with the string and start to wrap it around itself until it coils up into a smaller, denser string. Like that.

In order to create a karyotype like the one seen above, a medical professional will usually take a blood sample from you, separate out the white blood cells, put a few of them under a microscope with a camera attached, wait for **anaphase** of **mitosis** (that's when chromosomes separate the most), and then snap a picture. The picture comes up on a computer screen. The medical professional can then put your chromosomes together in an orderly karyotype, like the one seen above.

Humans have 23 pairs of chromosomes, under normal conditions. Some genetic disorders, such as Turner's syndrome or Down's syndrome, can result in a different chromosome number. However, most people have 23 pairs, or 46 chromosomes. The first 22 pairs are called autosomes because they are not associated with gender. The last pair are called the sex chromosomes. They are associated with gender (XX – female) (XY – male). They are usually placed at the end of the karyotype (as seen above), but are sometimes seen off to the side.

The karyotype above is a male. The last set of chromosomes has one larger chromosome (X) and one much smaller chromosome (Y). Since this person has 46 chromosomes total, we can tell that this male does not have Down's syndrome, Klinefelter's syndrome, or Edward's syndrome as those genetic disorders are all associated with having more than 46 chromosomes in humans.

The really cool thing about your karyotype is that it is the complete and total genetic book of you. In that one picture, is the information for the color of your eyes, how tall you will be, if you have large ears, or any genetic diseases that may arise in your lifetime. It can tell if you will be bald, when that may occur, when your hair will turn gray, and if you can taste certain chemicals.

The bad news about your karyotype is that currently we don't know how to read it very well. We have only started to translate it. The whole thing is written in 4 letters: A for adenine, T for thymine, C for cytosine, and G for guanine – these are the four nitrogenous bases of DNA and we will discuss them more in the DNA story. In 1990, a project called the **Human Genome Project** was started to *sequence* the human DNA; that is, to find out what all the letters are. We now know what all the letters are.

However, we have just started to learn what those letters *mean*. Some of the letters come together as "recipes" for proteins. There are recipes for your hair pigment, ear wax, and digestive enzymes, to name a few. Other letters seem to tell the cells when to start making the proteins – when to start producing growth hormone, for instance. Does your adolescent growth spurt start at age 11 or age 22? It's all in the karyotype! Still other letters will tell when to stop making the protein (does your hair pigment stop being produced at age 22 or 92?). There are, however, still many sequences of bases (letters) that we just don't know how to read yet. That's one of the exciting things about biology – there is still so much to do!

Sciency Words

Karyotype – an individual's collection of chromosomes. The term also refers to a laboratory technique that produces an image of an individual's chromosomes, and to the picture produced with the technique.

Nuclear membrane – a double membrane enclosing a cell nucleus. Its outer part is continuous with the endoplasmic reticulum. It is also called **nuclear** envelope.

Chromosome – the things that make organisms what they are. They carry all the information used to help a cell grow, thrive, and reproduce. Chromosomes are made up of DNA. Segments of DNA in specific patterns are called genes. You will find the chromosomes, the genetic material, in the nucleus of a cell.

Mitosis – a part of the cell cycle when replicated chromosomes are separated into two new nuclei. Cell division gives rise to genetically identical cells in which the number of chromosomes is maintained.

Anaphase – the fourth phase of mitosis. Anaphase is the process that separates the duplicated genetic material carried in the nucleus of a parent cell into two identical daughter cells. The separated chromosomes are then pulled to opposite poles of the cell.

Human Genome Project – (HGP) was an international scientific research project. The goal was to determine the base pairs that make up human DNA and to identify and map all the genes of the human karyotype, or genome.

Story #10: Twins and Eggs (Mitosis and Meiosis)

Mitosis

Mitosis is how most cells divide, reproduce, and make more cells. Mitosis produces a cell that is a clone of its parent cell. The word "mitosis" has the letter "T" in it and so does the word "twin." In mitosis, the cell makes a "twin," or exact copy of itself. Each cell in humans divides about every 24 hours so that is a lot of cell division!

There is no need to have genetic diversity in your liver cells or bone cells. You need your liver and bone cells (and most other cells in your body) to be the same two days from now as they are right now. You do not want any genetic diversity there. Therefore, the cell just makes a clone, or exact copy, of itself.

Let's look at the cell life cycle.

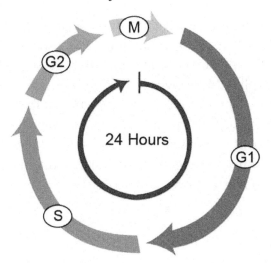

Cell Life Cycle

- G1 – this is cell growth. The cell is growing and doing whatever it is the cell is supposed to be doing such as producing hair pigment or engulfing bacteria.
- S – in this phase the DNA is copied. There are now two exact copies of the DNA per cell.
- G2 – more growth and normal cell life.
- M – mitosis. The cell divides. Each new cell gets one complete set of DNA, 46 chromosomes, and the cycle starts over again. There are 4 stages to mitosis: prophase, metaphase, anaphase, and telophase.
- Cytokinesis – the process by which a new cell membrane forms and the two new cells completely divide. This is considered separate from mitosis.

At this point, the whole cell cycle starts over again.

Meiosis

Meiosis is the process in which **sex cells** divide. In humans this only happens in egg cells and sperm cells. We do not want all our offspring to be genetically identical. This is where we want to see some genetic diversity. Therefore, each egg cell only receives half of our genetic information, in humans, 23 chromosomes. The same is true for sperm cells. Note that there is no letter "T" in meiosis. This process does **not** make twin cells. Each cell is unique. Meiosis is the reason that we genetically differ from our biological siblings no matter how many of them we have.

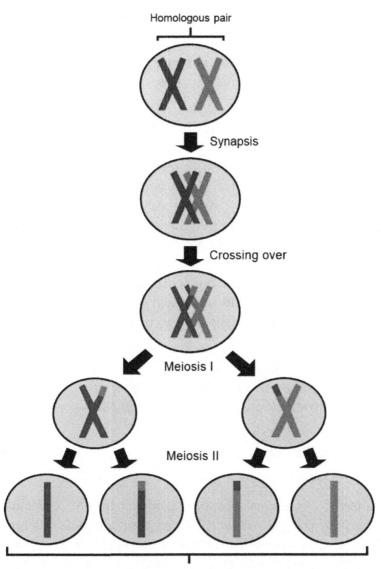

Four genetically distinct haploid daughter cells
(middle two are recombinants)

The exception to this is identical twins. Identical twins split apart early from the same fertilized egg. Therefore, they are genetically identical. Studying identical twins is a great way to study how different lifestyles and environments may affect genetic traits.

There are two main parts of meiosis; Meiosis I and Meiosis II. Each of these parts goes through prophase, metaphase, anaphase, and telophase. The most important differences between mitosis and meiosis occur during prophase I of meiosis I.

Look at the diagram to your left. The top cell, which could be an egg or a sperm cell, is showing two chromosomes, one of which you received from your biological mother and the other which you received from your biological father. In prophase I of meiosis I, during a process called **crossing over,** certain areas of the two chromosomes begin to switch with one another. You will notice in the diagram how some of the areas of the pink chromosome switch places with some of the areas of the blue chromosome. After crossing over occurs, each chromosome will go into a newly formed **haploid cell**. Haploid cells only occur in sex cells.

- Diploid cell – has the full number of chromosomes. In humans this is 46.
- Haploid cell – has half the number of chromosomes. In humans this is 23.

Sharing the Cookbook

It is time for a story.

Mitosis: *Remember Grandma's golden family cookbook? This is all of the DNA found in a cell, your complete and total family cookbook. All the recipes for everything from appetizers to desserts are there. As it comes time for you to leave your family home and start a home of your own, Grandma begins to make a complete copy (twin) of the family cookbook for you to take with you. This would be like in the cell cycle during the S-phase when the cell makes a complete copy of the DNA. Then when you leave the home, you have a complete and total cookbook to take with you. This is what happens in mitosis.*

Meiosis: *Meiosis would be more like the following. You and your brother are leaving home at the same time. Grandma has only one copy of the golden family cookbook, so she tears it in half. You get the appetizer half and your brother gets the dessert half. You each have half of a cookbook. Before you each leave to start your separate households, you exchange a few recipes. Maybe you swap your buffalo wing recipe for his brownie recipe. After 3 or so swaps, you each go your separate ways. This is more like meiosis.*

The swapping of recipes is like the crossing over of prophase I of meiosis I and *you each end up with only half of the recipe book.* This is how an egg cell ends up with 23 chromosomes and a sperm cell ends up with 23 chromosomes. When the two combine during fertilization, the resulting embryo gets 46.

Sciency Words

Sex cells (gametes) – an organism's reproductive cells. Female sex cells are called ova or egg cells, and male sex cells are called sperm. Sex cells are haploid cells; each cell carries only one copy of each chromosome.

Crossing over – the swapping of genetic material that occurs in the sex cells. During the formation of egg and sperm cells, also known as meiosis, paired chromosomes from each parent align so that similar DNA sequences from the paired chromosomes **cross over** one another.

Diploid cell – a cell with the full number of chromosomes. In humans this is 46, under normal circumstances.

Haploid cell – a sex cell with half the number of chromosomes. In humans this is 23, under normal circumstances.

Story #11: Baking is Easy to Understand Because Cookies are Delicious – Part 2 (DNA, RNA, & Protein Synthesis)

DNA, RNA, & Protein Synthesis

Your DNA (deoxyribonucleic acid) is the complete and total genetic book of you. Scientists sequenced all the nitrogen base letters (A – adenine, T – thymine, G – guanine, and C – cytosine) during the Human Genome Project (1990–2003). Some of those letters we now know how to read and interpret. However, there are still many more areas we have yet to learn. Almost every cell in your body has a complete and total copy of all of your DNA which makes up all 46 of your chromosomes. Each cell in your body only reads and uses a small amount of the information contained in the DNA. Your muscle cells, for example, need the recipes for the muscle proteins actin and myosin. Every time you are building more muscle tissue, or replacing worn out muscle tissue, the recipes for actin and myosin need to be read and those proteins need to be produced. Your muscle cells will never need to produce digestive enzymes or hair pigment, and yet muscle cells contain that information.

This is like your complete and total golden family cookbook. You may use some recipes, like your favorite chili, over and over again. There may be other recipes (hello fruitcake!) that you never use, but it has still been copied over and over again in the history of your family. Maybe your cousin has a copy of the family cookbook and uses the fruitcake recipe all the time.

As I have mentioned before, the golden family cookbook can never leave the kitchen during normal functions. Since the complete cookbook cannot leave, a copy of each recipe has to be made in order to take it to the ribosome, I mean kitchen, so the protein can be produced.

During normal cell life (not mitosis) the DNA cannot leave the nucleus of the cell. Remember that during mitosis, the nuclear membrane dissolves and the DNA then floats freely in the cytoplasm of the cell. So, during normal cell life, the mRNA (messenger RNA) – think of it like a train – enters the nucleus, opens the DNA to the recipe to be copied, copies it, closes the DNA and exits the nucleus. The mRNA then takes the information to the **ribosome**, where the protein will be produced.

This is like you making a copy or taking a picture of a recipe. You enter the kitchen (nucleus), open the cookbook to the correct page, take the picture (transcription), close the cookbook and return it to its proper spot, exit the kitchen, and take the recipe to the location where you need it.

Note that you do not have to copy the whole cookbook! This is not the copying of ALL the DNA. That occurs during the S-phase of cell life. This is only the copying of that ONE recipe. Much like a family cookbook, DNA has areas that mark the beginning of a recipe for a protein and the end of the recipe for that protein. Besides the ingredients for the protein, the DNA also has instructions on for example when to start making the protein and when to stop making the protein.

Look at the diagram below. Here you see the mRNA strand inside of a ribosome within the cell. The mRNA has the recipe for a protein written on it in the four letters, or nitrogen bases.

IMPORTANT NOTE: Three of the four nitrogen bases (adenine, guanine, and cytosine) are the same in both DNA and RNA. However, DNA also has the nitrogen base T – thymine. In RNA, all thymine is replaced by the nitrogen base U – uracil. This is good news for biology students because you can always tell if a problem or question is referring to DNA or RNA.

DNA example: TGCATGCAGAGCAACG. We know it's DNA because it has the "T" – thymine.

RNA example: ACGUACGUCUCGUUGC. We know it's RNA because it has a "U" – uracil – and no "T."

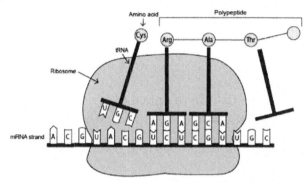

The above diagram shows the process of **protein synthesis**, or the creation of a protein. The recipe for a protein was copied from the DNA and brought to the ribosome by mRNA.

Complementary Pairs

The way that mRNA transcribes (or copies) a recipe from the DNA is by using **complementary pairs.** There are four nitrogen bases in DNA. The bases always pair up with A (adenine) bonding with T (thymine) and C (cytosine) bonding with G (guanine).

DNA:

- A with T (these bond with 2 weak hydrogen bonds)
- C with G (these bond with 3 weak hydrogen bonds)

To remember this, I think of the word "at." It is A with T and is a **2**-letter word – they bond with **2** weak hydrogen bonds.

RNA:

- A with U (remember, no "T" in RNA, it is replaced with "U" (uracil))
- C with G

Codons

- So, if the DNA in the nucleus read: TACCATGAT
- The mRNA would copy it as: AUGGUACUA

The mRNA would then take that information to the ribosome.

In order to make the protein, the transcript is read in groups of three letters. Each of these 3-letter groups is called a **codon**.

So, we break the mRNA up like this:

AUGGUACUA > AUG. GUA CUA

Each group of 3 is a codon. The first codon (AUG) is the *start codon*. Without this combination of letters, the protein will not be made because it cannot start. The start codon also codes for the **amino acid** (remember that these are the building blocks of protein, so that makes sense) **methionine**. Therefore, the first amino acid in **every** protein is always methionine. Sometimes the resulting protein keeps the methionine as a final ingredient and sometimes the resulting protein drops the methionine, however, methionine is always the first amino acid in every growing protein.

Look at the chart below. You will see that if you look up AUG, that it says, "START." It also has the amino acid methionine listed. So, at AUG the protein will start being made and methionine is the first ingredient in this protein.

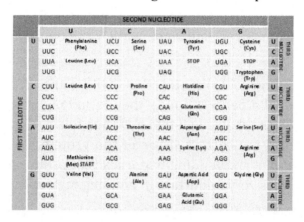

Codon chart.

Let's go back to our initial mRNA (**AUGGUACUA**), which we broke up into codons like this:

AUGGUACUA > AUG GUA CUA

We have now dealt with the **AUG.** The AUG is the start codon, which codes for methionine. Next, we have **GUA.** In referencing the above codon chart, we see that **GUA** codes for the amino acid valine. Valine is thus the second ingredient in our growing protein chain. Our third and final codon is **CUA.** Referencing the codon chart, we will see that **CUA** codes for leucine. So here is what our growing protein chain looks like so far:

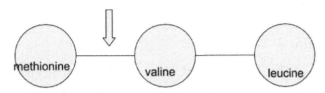

Peptide bond

Amino acids linked by peptide bonds start to form a protein.

There are 20 different types of amino acids. Some we can produce ourselves, and some we have to obtain from the food we eat.

As the amino acids link together (with a special covalent bond called a peptide bond), they form long polypeptide chains. These chains will fold and then fold again to eventually form the correct shape of the protein. Remember that proteins are building materials (hair, skin, enzymes) and shape is very important in building materials.

So, that's it! That's how the information that is locked in your golden family cookbook is copied, taken to the baking site, and made into a protein! Happy baking!

Sciency Words

Ribosome – macromolecular machines, found within all living cells, which perform biological protein synthesis. Ribosomes link amino acids together, in the order specified by the codons of messenger RNA molecules, forming polypeptide chains.

Transcription – the process by which the information in a strand of DNA is copied into a new molecule of messenger RNA (mRNA).

Protein Synthesis – the process in which cells make proteins. The first stage of the process is transcription. Transcription is the transfer of genetic instructions in DNA to mRNA in the nucleus. After a polypeptide chain is synthesized, it may undergo additional processing to form the finished protein.

Complementary pairs – the phenomenon where in DNA guanine always hydrogen bonds to cytosine and adenine always hydrogen bonds to thymine. The G–C bond shares 3 hydrogen bonds, while the A–T bond shares 2 hydrogen bonds.

Codon – a sequence of three DNA or RNA nucleotides that corresponds with a specific amino acid or stop signal during protein synthesis.

Amino Acid – an organic compound. It serves as a building block for proteins.

Methionine – an essential amino acid. It is a specific amino acid in that it is the first one to be incorporated into protein chains by the ribosome. For humans it is obtained from the diet, from for example seeds, meat, and fish.

STORY #12: A RECIPE COPIED WRONG (MUTATIONS)

Some Words About Mutations

What if the recipe is copied wrong? One of three things will occur.

1. *The recipe is so terrible that it cannot be used.*
2. *There is no difference to the outcome.*
3. *The recipe is better than the original.*

This depends on where in the recipe the mistake occurred, how bad of a mistake it was, and how important the involved ingredient was. For example, in a brownie recipe, if the recipe calls for 2 cups of **sugar** and you copy it incorrectly to say 2 cups of **salt**, that is a disaster! Those will be some terrible brownies that no one will ever eat! If the original recipe calls for **2** teaspoons of salt, and you copied incorrectly to say **1** teaspoon, that will not be a big deal. No one will probably even notice. However, if the original recipe calls for **1/2 cup** of chocolate chips and you copy it incorrectly to say **1 cup** of chocolate chips, that may be better! You may keep that recipe!

Occasionally, when DNA is being copied during the S-phase of mitosis, or when mRNA is copying a recipe from the DNA during transcription, a mistake is made. Any mistake in the copying of the DNA is called a **mutation**.

There are all kinds of mutations. There can be a **deletion**, where a section of the DNA goes missing. There can be an **insertion**, where extra sections of DNA are added in. **Substitutions** occur when nucleotide sequences are incorrect.

For example, in the genetic disorder *sickle cell anemia*, CTT becomes CAT in one section of one chromosome (chromosome 11). This causes the amino acid valine to substitute in for the amino acid glutamic acid. This change in only one nucleotide causes the red blood cells to sickle (become crescent-shaped), rather than their normal bi-concave shape.

There are many other types of mutations.

We usually think of mutations as bad, as in the case of sickle cell anemia or cystic fibrosis. However, mutations can also be beneficial. A genetic mutation in arctic bears many thousands of years ago caused some of them to appear white. This turned out to be an incredible advantage in their snowy environment as they were able to hunt more prey, grow quicker, and overall have better health. The bears that did not have this advantage were forced to move further south in order to survive. As the two groups of bears started to live in different regions, eventually they grew apart to the point where they can no longer breed and have viable offspring with one another. At that point, we would say that the two populations of bears have become two different **species** of bears: polar bears and brown bears. So, mutations can be beneficial, and can even lead to the evolution of new species.

Most mutations, however, are not noticed. They may not make a difference in the amino acid being coded for, or the protein they make isn't life altering. For example, perhaps your original DNA coded for a dimple in your chin and because of a mutation you have no chin dimple. Scientists have calculated that the average human has 60 genetic mutations. Thankfully, most of those are neutral, or not life threatening. Maybe you've even got some beneficial ones that make learning biology much easier! Hey – we can hope!

Sciency Words

Mutation – an alteration in the nucleotide sequence of the genome of an organism.

Deletion – a type of **mutation** involving the loss of genetic material. It can be small, involving a single missing DNA base pair, or large, involving a piece of a chromosome.

Insertion – a type of **mutation** involving the addition of genetic material. An **insertion mutation** can be small, involving a single extra DNA base pair, or large, involving a piece of a chromosome.

Substitution – a type of **mutation** where one base pair is replaced by a different base pair. The term also refers to the replacement of one amino acid in a protein with a different amino acid.

Species – a group of organisms that can reproduce with one another in nature and produce fertile offspring.

STORY #13: BEES ARE MEAN (THE NATURE OF SCIENCE)

A Story on the Nature of Science

When I was a teenager, I was washing the outside windows at my grandmother's house. As I stood on a low ladder, I must have angered a bee because it began flying into my face. No amount of swatting did any good to get rid of this bee! Now, I don't really care for bees and certainly didn't want to get stung, so I got down from the ladder and attempted to run away from the bee. At first, I ran around a tree. However, the bee was still flying at me and being pretty aggressive. Then I ran around the whole house! I stopped a bit at certain places, hoping I had lost the bee. No such luck. That bee followed me around the entire house! I decided it was time for a break and went inside. I got a snack and went to sit on the couch and watch some MTV (it was the 80s, that's what we did). After about an hour, my grandmother was wanting me to finish the windows so I went back outside. Now, several people had been in and out of the house in the last hour with no incident, but as soon as I walked outside, a bee landed on my finger and stung me! That bee waited for me for over an hour and stung me as soon as I walked outside!

Science, at the time, said that bees have a very simple brain and can, at most, remember a person for a few seconds. In this case, I do not care what science says. That bee waited for ME and stung ME. It was the same bee. It remembered. It waited.

Science might say that it was perhaps another bee. That I had perfume or food on my shirt that attracted bees. That it was a coincidence. Again, I say, it doesn't matter to me in this case what science says. That bee remembered me. That bee was mean. This is my personal experience and I'll stick to it all of my life. Because it happened to me.

****

I'm going to say something here that may surprise you. Science does not have all the answers. I'll say it again. Science does not have all the answers.

Furthermore, science has rules. Those rules must be followed for something to be considered science. Here are the rules:

- The results are public and objective.
- The results are consistent.
- The results are observable.
- The explanation is based on natural laws.
- The results are predictable.
- The results are testable.
- The results are tentative.

Some questions that are important in our lives simply cannot be answered in a scientific way. Questions like, "what is love?," "what makes something beautiful?," "is there an afterlife?," "is rock or classical music better?"

Science is one way that we learn about the universe and our place in it. It is a great way to learn about the universe and our place in it, but it is not the only way. There are other ways of knowing. Let's discuss a few.

Personal Experience

The story about the bee is my personal experience. I was there. It happened to me. I *believe* that the bee remembered me for over an hour, recognized me, and stung me in revenge for my washing the window too near them. Could this be turned into a scientific question? Perhaps. We would have to set up an experiment that tested bee's ability to remember. We would have to be able to test many bees and get consistent results over and over again. Then those results would have to be published so that other scientists can redo the experiments and get the same results. The scientific community agrees that if better information is found in the future, our results could be modified or proven altogether wrong.

Some people have personal experiences that science cannot deal with. For instance, there is a famous baker whose father passed away when he was nineteen. The family had expected this young man to take over the bakery, but now he was forced to do it much earlier than expected while still grieving over the death of his father. The whole family was depending on him. Now, there was this one particularly hard-to-make pastry that was a specialty of the bakery. The young man tried several times to make it but failed. He felt that the whole family was watching him and that if he could not get this pastry right, he would be failing them. Once, he stayed at the bakery until very late at night trying to get the dough just right – failing once again. Dejected, he went home and fell asleep on his couch. As he slept, he tells that his recently deceased father appeared to him in a dream and showed him how to make the dough. The young man woke early, went to the bakery, and made the dough correctly. He *believes* that his father came to him in that dream to help him succeed.

Can we make this science? Do we want to? Does the baker care? Probably not.

We cannot replicate this experience. Yes, we could hook up probes and tell if the baker is dreaming. We cannot know *what* he is dreaming. We can *believe* him or not. There is no way to test this or have it be predictable. Even if we could know what his dream was about, there is no way to set up an experiment to tell if it was his father appearing from the beyond, or simply repressed memories surfacing in a stressful time. This story is not science. These are not questions that science can answer. They are part of this young man's **personal experience**. He probably doesn't care much about the science involved.

There are people who have claimed to have near death experiences, to have seen fantastic sea creatures, or to have witnessed UFOs. Science always says, "Prove it." If one can give consistent, observable, natural, predictable, testable proof that is made open to public, objective scrutiny, *then it is science.*

Personal experience is not science. That does not mean it is not real or valuable. It is just not science.

Intuition

Intuition is another way that we can know about something. If you were to go to the teacher about your classmate and you told the teacher you are getting weird vibes from this kid, the teacher would probably ask you for evidence. "Did he say something to you? Did he trip you? Threaten you? Give you a dirty look?" "No", you say, "I'm just getting a weird feeling." Your teacher would not be able to do much about this except be on the lookout for anything wrong. And yet police officers will tell you that if you feel something is wrong, your intuition is often correct.

Sometimes we meet someone and just know that we will be good friends. And then we are! Intuition is a way that we know about our world. It is just not science.

Religion

Historically, this has been a pretty hot topic. Please do not worry. There are many ways to know if something is true or not. Religion and science (along with personal experience and intuition) are different ways to discover if something is true or not. Faith, by definition, is *believing* something without proof. Science, by definition, says, "prove it." Let's take a question we would all like an answer to. Is there an afterlife? Science cannot deal with this question because scientists would either have to prove that there was an afterlife, or prove that there is not an afterlife. Science can't do that.

We can't set up experiments that test this process over and over again. Even if we could, we would not be dealing with natural laws or getting observable results. World religions, however, can and do deal with this question all the time. Again, faith is *believing* something without proof. Your religious views, or lack of religious views, are based on intuition, scripture study, meditation, prayer, and association with other believers. Your religious views are personal (subjective), not up for public scrutiny (objective). Most religious people do not think their faith should be testable or tentative. Religion is a different way of knowing. Studying religious and philosophical questions is an important and valuable part of life. It is just not science. And that is okay.

Science

So, just what sorts of questions can science address? Well, ones that can be proven in a consistent, observable, natural, predictable, testable, tentative, public, and objective way. "Salmon avoid warm waters." That is a hypothesis that science can test and either prove or disprove. "Vaccine A will prevent the flu." That can be tested. If we find evidence that that is not true, we will toss it out and start again. Science is okay with being wrong. That is actually how science works.

Let me give you an example: There were once dinosaur bones discovered. All evidence led the scientists to accept that this dinosaur had a nose spike! That was an exciting discovery! A statue of this dinosaur was even constructed in New York's Central Park. Wealthy people could have dinner inside the statue. Then more fossils of this dinosaur were found and more scientists studied them. This new evidence showed that the bone once thought to be a nose spike was actually a thumb. The early science was wrong. That's okay! More than okay – it's *exciting* when science is wrong! Science is tentative and can always change with new evidence. That is the way that science works. Otherwise, we would all be carrying around huge phones from the 1980s!

Side note: The Iguanodon statues in New York's Central Park have long been destroyed. Here's an image of the incorrect iguanodon statues, nose spike and all, which are now in London.

STORY #14: HAROLD AND STANLEY TACKLE LIFE (ORIGIN OF LIFE)

How Did Life Start?

The quick answer is: we don't know.

That, however, has not stopped us from trying to find out! Of course, the other ways of knowing (religion, intuition, personal experience, meditation, etc.) all have many ways to ask and ponder this basic question, and that is valid and good. **Science** has also taken on this question.

First, the Basics

Our solar system is approximately 5 billion years old, with Earth itself a bit younger at 4.6 billion years. Based on the age of rocks, and microfossils and trapped gases found in those rocks, we know some things about the conditions of early Earth.

It was hot. There were gases such as ammonia (NH_3), hydrogen (H_2), methane (CH_4), and water vapor (H_2O) in the atmosphere. There were hot, shallow seas covering much of the Earth. There was no ozone layer and not much atmosphere. There was little oxygen (O_2). There were storms with lightning, intense radiation from the young sun, and a lot of water condensation and evaporation going on. Some people have come to call these conditions the "primordial soup" of early Earth.

Anyhow, back in 1923 there was a Russian scientist by the name of Alexander I. Oparin who wrote a *one-page* paper that put forth the following idea: with the conditions of early Earth, along with a power source such as lightning or intense ultraviolet (UV) radiation, macromolecules such as protein could have arisen.

That was it. One page.

"Prove It!"

Most scientists of his day agreed that this was plausible. But you know what science always says: "Prove it!" Well, Oparin couldn't prove it. He was living in Russia in 1923 and there was no way to simulate in a lab the type of intense UV radiation or lightning strikes that would have been required. So that was it.

But wait! We now have ways to simulate intense radiation and lightning in a lab! We should try it! Well, that's exactly what Stanley Miller and Harold Urey did in their very famous Miller and Urey experiment of 1952. Here's what they did: They got some water boiling in a condensation chamber. They collected water vapor (the gaseous state of water – you know, steam), and drove it into a chamber with varying amounts of ammonia gas, hydrogen gas, and methane. They used an electrode to shock these gases, which simulated the lightning. They then cooled the gases and hoped for some signs of life.

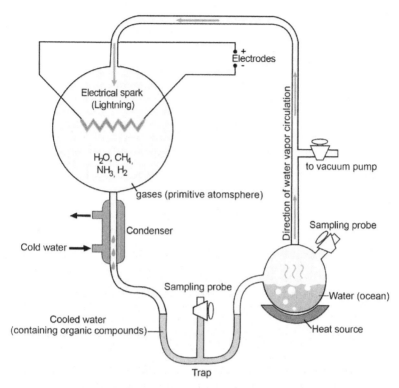

Miller and Urey's experimental apparatus.

What were the results of this experiment?

Well, they got some nucleic acids (the instructions for life), amino acids (building blocks of life), ATP (adenosine triphosphate – the energy source for life), and some other complicated gunk that scientists are still trying to work out!

Interesting.

So, they got the instructions for life, the building blocks of life, and the energy source for life. Did they create life? No. Miller and Urey were successful in creating some of the ingredients for life, but they **did not** create life. They got no cells.

This is frustrating. It is a lot like going to look at the construction site where you want to build your dream home. The workers are there. The building materials are there. The blueprint is there. And yet, your house is not being built. Why not? It should work! But it doesn't.

Doesn't this almost make you want to set up your own experiment and see if YOU could create a cell, or bacteria, or life out of these simple gases? Maybe if you just added more water, or left out the ammonia, or doubled the UV radiation, or cooled it all down quicker – then you could discover the secret of how life came to be! A lot of scientists have done exactly these things and more and still, as of today, we have yet to create "life" out of "not life." The third part of the cell theory stands. All cells come from pre-existing cells.

****

It is interesting and important to note that some meteorites (space rocks that hit Earth) have also contained organic matter, such as amino acids. So, there are some hypotheses that state that maybe life didn't start on Earth, but instead started elsewhere in the universe and traveled here on space debris.

SIDE STORY #14B: MY CELLS ATE OTHER CELLS AND NOW THERE ARE BACTERIA INSIDE MY CELLS?!?! (ENDOSYMBIOSIS)

Endosymbiosis

- "Endo" – within.
- "Symbiosis" – living together.

What about us? How did our cells, eukaryotic cells, first come to be? As mentioned in the title of this essay, that is quite a story!

However life started, microfossils here on Earth indicate that the first life were one-celled prokaryotes[8]. These organisms are called archaea. They appeared roughly 3.5 billion years ago, which is quite soon after the formation of Earth. Eukaryotes (organisms whose cells contain a nucleus and membrane-bound organelles) arrived about a billion years later, 2.7 billion years ago.

Here's how those first eukaryotes came to be: A primitive prokaryote came to live inside a larger prokaryote. The larger prokaryote probably tried to eat the smaller one through the process of phagocytosis. The smaller prokaryote, however, was very good at converting glucose into energy. So, they came to live together. The smaller prokaryote gave the larger one more energy and the larger prokaryote protected the smaller one. With this protection, the smaller prokaryote was able to reproduce more and supply the larger cell with even more energy. Do you

---

[8] Remember: eukaryote cells contain a nucleus and membrane-bound organelles, while prokaryote cells do not.

know what that smaller prokaryote became? The **mito-chondria**! The cell organelle that turns glucose into our old friend ATP (adenosine triphosphate!). All this additional energy was very advantageous for life 2.7 billion years ago! This was the start of the first eukaryote.

Later, a photosynthetic bacterium (prokaryote) got inside of a pre-cell and produced food out of sunlight, which was beneficial to that cell. This prokaryote became the **chloro-plast** of photosynthetic, eukaryotic cells.

These are both examples of **endosymbiosis** – a type of symbiosis in which one organism lives inside the other, the two typically behaving as a single organism. It is believed to be how such organelles as mitochondria and chloro-plasts arose within eukaryotic cells.

That is a very nice hypothesis, but you know what science always says: Prove it!

Okay.

Evidence of Endosymbiosis

1. Both mitochondria and chloroplasts replicate inde-pendently of the rest of the cell. That whole mitosis thing? It doesn't affect them at all. Mitochondria and chloroplasts reproduce whenever they want.

2. Both mitochondria and chloroplasts contain their own DNA, and this DNA differs from the rest of the cell. So, in addition to your 46 regular chromosomes in the nucleus, you also have **mitochondrial DNA**. A lot of interesting re-search is being done on mitochondrial DNA.

- Mitochondrial and chloroplast DNA is shaped as a circle. This is called a **plasmid** and is a characteristic of bacterial DNA.

Sciency Words

Mitochondria – organelles within eukaryotic cells that produce adenosine triphosphate (ATP), the main energy molecule used by the cell.

Chloroplast – a cell organelle that produces energy through photosynthesis.

Mitochondrial DNA – although most DNA is packaged in chromosomes within the nucleus, mitochondria also have a small amount of their own DNA. This genetic material is known as mitochondrial DNA or mtDNA.

Plasmid – a small, circular, double-stranded DNA molecule that is distinct from a cell's chromosomal DNA. Plasmids naturally exist in bacterial cells.

STORY #15: THE POLAR BEAR BROTHERS (NATURAL SELECTION)

Evolution by Means of Natural Selection

Imagine, if you will, two polar bear brothers born this morning in the arctic. One, because of random expression of inherited traits, has brown fur. The other one, also because of random expression of inherited traits, has fur that appears white. The polar bear brothers live in a snowy environment in which it is increasingly difficult to find food. As they grow and mature, the bears learn to hunt seals, birds, and fish. Under these circumstances, with one brown bear and one white bear in the snowy arctic, which polar bear blends in with his environment more? The white one. Which polar bear will be more successful in hunting and feeding? The white one. Which polar bear will grow faster and stronger, survive to reproduce, and attract the healthier mate? Again, the white polar bear that blends into the snowy environment. It is a sadder story for the brown polar bear. Because he does not blend in as well, he has a harder time securing food. This may mean that he does not survive long enough to pass his genes on to offspring. Or, if he does survive, his offspring may not be as healthy due to lack of food. This is why we don't find many brown polar bears, they don't survive to pass their genes on to the next generation.

But let's change the story.

Imagine, if you will, two polar bear brothers born this morning in the arctic. One, because of random expression of inherited traits, has brown fur. The other one, also because of random expression of inherited traits, has fur that allows

113

*it to appear white. The polar bear brothers live in a snowy environment in which it is increasingly difficult to find food. Tonight, there will be a large volcanic eruption in the arctic. This eruption will cover the area in brown ash which will persist for many years to follow. Now, under **these** circumstances, which polar bear blends in with his environment more? The brown one. Which polar bear will be more successful in hunting and feeding? The brown one. Which polar bear will grow faster and stronger, survive to reproduce, and attract the healthier mate? Again, the brown bear that blends into the environment. This time it is a sad story for the white polar bear. A white polar bear in a brown environment will stand out and not be able to hunt. He will probably not survive to pass those genes on to the next generation.*

Genetics Are Random

Genetics are random. Flip of the coin. Luck of the draw. What are the odds of being born female or male? 50/50 – random. Why did you get curly hair and your sister has straight hair? Again, random. Why was one polar bear brother born with brown fur and another with white fur? Again, it's random. One gene goes into one egg cell, or sperm cell, while another gene goes to another. We call these random, inheritable changes.

Natural Selection in NOT Random

The genetic changes are random (brown fur vs. white fur). However, how nature will select these traits is *not* random. We can predict the traits that nature will choose, they depend on the environment. Nature will choose those traits that allow an organism to survive, obtain resources, and find a healthy mate to allow them to pass on those traits. How do we know which polar

bear brother will be stronger, healthier, and survive to pass on his traits? It depends on the environment.

A big, heavy beak for a nut-eating bird is an advantage in years when walnuts have thick shells. Birds with big, heavy beaks are more likely to crack open the shells and be able to eat more walnuts. However, in seasons when walnuts have thin shells, a big, heavy beak is just, well, heavy.

So, genetic variations within a population are random. How nature "selects" one characteristic over another depends on the environment. This is how natural selection works. It makes a population of organisms that are better suited to their environment. As the environment changes, so does the characteristics that make an individual more fit.

"Fit"

Charles Darwin put up the theory of evolution by means of natural selection in his book *On the Origin of Species by Means of Natural Selection*. His definition of "fitness" was that an organism with high fitness would survive to pass their genes onto the next generation, while those with low fitness would not survive or reproduce as successfully.

Charles Darwin did not coin the phrase, "survival of the fittest." We think a philosopher by the name of Herbert Spencer first said that, but it has been said a lot. Actually, it is not true. At least not in natural selection. You do not have to be the "fittest" to pass your genes onto the next generation. How fit do you have to be? "Fit enough."

For example, in humans, it is not only the Olympic champions that get to pass on their Olympic champion genes to the next generation. Thankfully, for most of us, we do not have to be the strongest, fastest, best-looking, or richest to pass on our genes. We do not need to be the "fittest." How fit do we have to be? *Fit enough!* As long as we are healthy enough to survive to the age of reproduction and then healthy enough to produce sex cells (egg or sperm) and have a child, then we are fit enough to pass our fit genes on to the next generation. Survival of those who are *fit enough!*

When many individuals in a population are fit enough to reproduce and have viable offspring (that means the offspring are also capable of reproducing), this gives a population a great genetic variety. In populations that reproduce sexually (that is, with a blending of genetic traits), this is a good thing. The more genetic variety a population has, the better that population is at dealing with a changing environment.

When I was first out of college, I worked at a well-known public aquarium that housed a large collection of sea anemones. Sea anemones are very simple animals in the Phylum Cnidaria that can reproduce sexually or asexually. They live in various aquatic ocean environments, often coral reefs and tide pools.

Sea anemone

What we informally observed at the aquarium was that when the sea anemones were healthy, they reproduced asexually. That is, they formed **buds** (which are genetic clones of the parent). We liked to see buds on the sea anemones. That meant they were feeling great and healthy. However, when doing routine checks of the water quality, if we found sea anemone eggs or sperm, that was a cause for concern. It seemed that sea anemones only reproduced sexually (that is produced egg and sperm) when they were under some sort of stress. Perhaps their water was too hot/cold, too much/not enough salt, too little current in the water, wrong type of food, etc. This was always a very interesting observation to me, and I've formed a hypothesis:

Sea anemones have been on Earth for about 500 million years. That's a long time and the Earth has changed a lot during those 500 million years.

If the parent anemone is healthy and well in its sea environment, then a clone offspring will probably also be healthy and well. No need for genetic variety. Might as well just produce a clone.

However, if the sea anemone is not healthy and well in that environment, reproducing sexually gives the resulting offspring more of a chance for survival. Because the parents will produce offspring with genetic variations, there is a better chance for at least some of those offspring to have traits that allow them to survive the changing conditions.

In the case of sea anemones, as well as any other organism that reproduces sexually, genetic variety is key in allowing a population to survive changing environmental conditions.

Did you get that? **Genetic variety is key** in allowing a population to **survive changing environmental conditions**.

And you thought we were just telling cute stories about polar bears and sea anemones.

Sciency Word

<u>Bud</u> – a prominence that develops into a new individual, sometimes permanently attached to the parent and sometimes becoming detached.

STORY #16: CLASSIFICATION FOR BIRDS (CLASSIFICATION)

Here are some birds. I like birds. Put these birds into groups. I'll wait.

If you are an avid birdwatcher or an **ornithologist** (a scientist who studies birds), putting these birds into groups was not hard. For most of us, however, this is a confusing task. What did I mean when I said to put the birds in groups? How many groups? What are the groups based on? Should we pick groups based on the size of the bird, the geographical range of the bird, how pretty the bird is?

These are precisely the types of questions that **taxonomists** deal with all of the time. **Taxonomy** is the science of naming, describing, and classifying organisms. **Taxonomists** can organize living things into groups by studying the morphological, behavioral, genetic, and biochemical characteristics of organisms.

There is such a huge variety of life, and we humans like to put things in groups to have some order. It makes all of life a lot easier to study if we have some sort of system in which to study it.

Back in the day (about 350 B.C.), Aristotle classified living things into 2 groups; "Plants" and "Animals." That was a good start. Aristotle then further divided "Animals" into 3 categories, "land," "air," and "water." This is where the problems started. For example, most of us would put birds into the "air" category. That leaves penguins to the "land" category, away from the rest of the birds. Then again, maybe penguins should be in the "water" category since they are such good swimmers and feed in the water. What about frogs? The adult frogs would be on "land" and the young frogs (tadpoles) would be in a different category ("water"). Where does that leave adolescent frogs?

Adolescent Frog

Penguin

These problems were taken on in the 1700s by Carl Linnaeus[9], also known as Carl von Linné[10]. He was a Swedish botanist, zoologist, and physician who formalized **binomial nomenclature**, the modern system of naming organisms. He is known as the "father of modern taxonomy." Here is the system Linnaeus set up, going from the largest to the smallest categories:

Kingdom

Phylum

Class

Order

Family

Genus

Species

There are a lot of mnemonic devices that help students remember this. I've always used, "King Phillip Came Over For Good Soup." (**K**ing – **King**dom. **P**hilip – **Ph**ylum. **Ca**me – **C**lass. **O**ver – **O**rder. **F**or – **F**amily. **G**ood – **G**enus. **S**oup – **S**pecies.) The system works like this:

Modern Human

Kingdom: Animalia
(we are not plants, fungi, or bacteria)

---

[9] Linnaeus was born "Carl von Linné." He liked his Latin naming system so much that he legally changed his name to its Latin version, Carolus Linnaeus.

[10] Linnaeus thought highly of himself. He is quoted as saying, "God created, Linnaeus ordered."

Phylum: Chordata
(we have a dorsal nerve cord; a *spinal cord*)

Class: Mammalia
(we have hair or fur, give birth to live young,
and produce milk)

Order: Primate
(hands with opposable thumbs and flat nails,
forward facing eyes)

Family: Hominidae
(no tails, well-developed forearms)

Genus: Homo
(large brain, walk upright)

Species: sapiens

The scientific name for a modern human is *Homo sapiens*. Note that this is the **genus** and **species** names put together. That is what Carolus Linnaeus meant by *binomial nomenclature*; it is a two-name naming system. Linnaeus chose to use Latin because it was considered the universal language by "learned" people at the time. Common names can be confusing: The rainbow trout is a fish found in freshwater throughout the world. The same species of fish is also called a steelhead by some and a coastal rainbow by others. This can be confusing. Using the Latin scientific name *Oncorhynchus mykiss*, scientists can be sure that they are all referring to the same fish.

Additions Since the 1700s

For the most part, we still use the system and structure set up by Linnaeus in the 1700s. However, some changes have taken place since then, and modifications have been made.

Divisions

One of these changes is the addition of Divisions. Division is a category even larger than Kingdom. There are 3 Divisions: Archaea (which includes prokaryotes that live in harsh conditions and are assumed to be some of the first organisms to live on Earth), Bacteria (prokaryotes that have different RNA and cells walls from the archaea), and Eukarya (all Eukaryotes, including Protists, Fungi, Plants, and Animals).

So, really the mnemonic device should be "**D**aring King Phillip Came Over For Good soup." Or something like that.

Morphology Versus Phylogeny

Woah! Those are some sciency words. Let me explain.

Morphology

Morphology is looking at the physical characteristics of an organism to determine its evolutionary relationship to other organisms. This is all that Carolus Linnaeus and other scientists had to work with. So, for example, the definition of a "Bird" is an animal characterized by feathers, toothless beaked jaws, the laying of hard-shelled eggs, a high metabolic rate, a four-chambered heart, and a strong yet lightweight skeleton. These are all characteristics we can directly observe.

Phylogeny

Then came DNA. DNA was described in the 1950s by Watson and Crick, but genetic testing was not widely used until the 1980s. Now taxonomists had a different, more accurate, tool in their toolboxes.

What we have learned by doing DNA and other genetic testing is that ...

... Carolus Linnaeus was good at his job.

He, along with other scientists since the 1770s, actually got it right most of the time! They were very good at using physical characteristics, such as beaks or heel bones, to figure out which organisms were more closely related to which other organisms.

Phylogeny is finding out how closely organisms are related by comparing **DNA or genetic or biochemical characteristics**. We are moving toward using this type of testing to learn more about life and where organisms should be placed. Modern science is now moving away from morphology (how something looks) and toward depending on phylogeny (an organism's evolutionary background).

A case in point is how closely birds are related to alligators and crocodiles. More testing is currently going on to determine when these animals may have shared a common ancestor. As new information becomes available, more adjustments will be made to the current classification system.

Some Words About "Species"

The definition of a *species* is a group of organisms that can reproduce with one another in nature and produce fertile offspring.

Two donkeys are able to reproduce with each other and create fertile offspring. That is a species.

A horse can reproduce with a donkey and a mule will be born. However, mules are sterile. Two mules cannot reproduce with each other. Mules are considered hybrids of horses and donkeys. Mules are not their own species. Because two horses can reproduce and have baby horses that can grow up to reproduce, horse is its own species.

That is the rule. Yet – we don't always follow our own rule.

For example, your domestic dog, *Canis lupus familiaris,* is considered a separate species from the coyote, *Canis latrans.* Yet these two organisms can reproduce with one another and have fertile offspring. According to our own rule, domestic dogs and coyotes should still be the same species and have the same scientific name. Yet, scientists have assigned them two different scientific names while they really should not, according to the definition of species.

This isn't the only case. A bottlenose dolphin has the scientific name *Tursiops truncatus.* A false killer whale has the scientific name *Pseudorca crassidens.* They are considered two distinct species. However: They can both be found in the waters surrounding Hawaii. There have been offspring that have been found to be half false killer whale and half bottlenose dolphin (a wholphin! I'm not kidding, that is what it is called!). These wholphin **are** able to reproduce (usually with another bottlenose dolphin) and have offspring. So, *technically*, according to our own definition, dolphins, and whales (at least these two) should be considered the same species and **not** have two separate scientific names.

There is also a problem with the definition of "species" for those organisms that reproduce asexually. Remember: our definition of species is a group of organisms that can reproduce with one another in nature and produce fertile offspring.

A sea sponge is an animal (albeit a simple animal) that can reproduce by being torn into pieces (asexually). Each piece then becomes a new individual that is a clone of the parent. According to NOAA (National Oceanic and Atmospheric Administration), there are approximately 8,550 species of sponges. Yet, how can we consider these separate species, according to our own definition? Sea sponges do not need to reproduce with one another. They can just clone themselves. So, there are some problems with the definition of "species."

Story #17: Big Moments in Animal Evolution

I could write a whole textbook about important things in biology. In fact, many, many people have. They are called biology textbooks. They are incredibly informative, but are very detailed. And long. **I don't want this book to be that long, so I have chosen to focus on the Big Moments in Animal Evolution.** I believe **these are** body cavities, the anus, the swim bladder, coming onto land, the amniotic egg, and endothermy. I will write some words about each.

Body Cavities

The major animal groups beginning with the simplest and moving to the most complex;

- Sponges/Porifera (no body cavity)
- Sea anemones, corals, jellies/Cnidaria (no body cavity)
- Flatworms/Platyhelminthes (no body cavity)
- Roundworms/Nematoda (partial body cavity)
- Rotifers/Rotifera (partial body cavity)
- Earthworms, leeches/Annelida (body cavity)
- Clams, snails, squid, octopus/Mollusca (body cavity)
- Arthropoda/ insects, spiders, crab, shrimp (body cavity)
- Fish, amphibians, reptiles, birds, mammals/Vertebrata (body cavity)

A body cavity cushions major organs while still allowing them to move. For instance, our lungs can expand and fill with air because they are not attached completely to the body wall, yet they remain protected inside our chest cavity. Humans are **coelomates**, which means we, along with Annelids, Mollusks, and all other vertebrates, have a fully lined body cavity, inside and out.

*Pretend you have a very special, delicate holiday ornament. Maybe it is a family heirloom. When you put it away after the holidays you take great care. You line a special container with tissue paper. Then you wrap the ornament itself in tissue paper also and put it inside the box. That is how the organs of coelomates are wrapped within the body cavity. There is a layer of tissue (epithelial tissue) that lines the inside of the body cavity. There is another layer of tissue that surrounds each internal organ or structure. That is why we say the coelomates have a **fully lined** body cavity, inside and out.*

Again, the main advantage of fully lined body cavities is that the organs are cushioned while still allowed movement.

There are 2 major groups of animals (roundworms and rotifers) that are **pseudocoelomates** (pseudo – "false" or "fake"). These are organisms that only have a partially lined body cavity.

Going back to the holiday ornament antidote, the ornament would be wrapped, but you would not have that extra layer of tissue paper lining the inside of the box.

Some animals do not have a body cavity at all. They are referred to as **acoelomates** – if you want to sound fancy.

These different types of body cavities relate to how the embryos of these animals develop. They show the progression of animal development from no body cavity, to a partially lined body cavity, to a fully lined body cavity. It is one of many examples of animals developing from simple to more complex.

The Anus

A jellyfish (or just jelly) is a predator. Larger jellyfish can sting and stun fish and then "walk" the fish slowly toward the mouth. They then take the prey into their body cavity where the fish will be digested. The bones, scales, and other indigestible waste products are released from the ... wait for it ... mouth. That's right, there is only one opening for the food to come in and the waste to exit. It is not the most efficient way to digest food, but it works for jellyfish. Sponges and flatworms also take in nutrients and release wastes from the same cells or tissues. All of this "only one opening for food and waste" arrangement changed for the roundworms (Nematoda). Evolution gave them an anus! That's right, they could take food into one opening and release it from a different opening. How convenient! More importantly, that is also much more efficient. Now digestion can be more of an assembly line production, where different nutrients can be absorbed in different areas along the digestive tract.

Earthworms took this a step further. They developed a really long intestine so that they could eat harder-to-digest things (like nutrients in soil). This allowed earthworms to grow much larger than the little roundworms. However, if animals were to grow even larger than earthworms, we had to find a way to digest efficiently *without* having to grow longer and longer. In the mollusks (clams, scallops, snails, slugs, squid, and octopus, to name a few), we see evolution tinkering with folding the intestine to make a longer intestine fit into a more compact body plan. *True story: the snail's anus is right over top of its head.* This plan seemed to have worked, as most vertebrates (except for snakes, they went back to the long body plan) have a twisted intestine. Our human small intestine is approximately 5 meters long! The large intestine, or colon, adds another twisted 1.5 meters. Just think of how tall we would have to be if our intestines didn't twist. Our long, twisted intestines allow us to eat a large variety of food and still digest it all rather efficiently. And the anus is a good thing, as well – unless you're a jellyfish.

The Swim Bladder

Another important adaptation in animal evolution is the swim bladder. This is also sometimes referred to as the gas bladder or air bladder and it is found in the fishes. The swim bladder is an internal organ and fills with gases to control the buoyancy, the ability to float, in most fish.

Think of it like this. It is a hot summer day and you are holding an inflated beach ball as you lie in your swimming pool. You decide that you would like to sink to the bottom of your pool for a moment. So, you pull the plug on the beach ball and deflate it. Because your bathing suit is weighted down (I don't know why), as you squeeze air out of the beach ball, you begin to sink to the bottom of the pool. While at the bottom of the pool, you decide it is time to rise back up to the surface. You begin to blow air back into the beach ball (you have incredible lung capacity). As you inflate the beach ball, you begin to rise back up in the water column until you are once again floating at the top of the pool. Now take this whole concept, but make the beach ball an internal structure. That is a swim bladder!

We often see a fish drawn with bubbles coming out of its mouth. This would be a fish that was deflating its swim bladder in order to sink in the water column. Not all fish have swim bladders. Sharks and rays do not. This makes it easier for sharks and rays to lie on the bottom of the ocean floor. However, it also means that they have to *swim* up and down in the water column. They cannot just *ascend* and *descend* like most other fish can.

What makes the swim bladder such an important moment in animal evolution? **It is the swim bladder that eventually evolved into lungs.**

Fish have gills. That is how they receive oxygen. There is a type of ancient fish called a lungfish. In this group of fish, we see both gills and lungs. Most lungfish live in areas of the world with a rainy season and a dry season. In the rainy season, they swim and use their gills to get oxygen. Then when the dry season comes, their lakes and ponds dry up. So, they burrow into the mud and go into a state of **estivation** (like hibernation this is a state of inactivity, but in the summer heat). The lungfish will then create a tube, made of mud, up to the surface. They are then able to use their lungs to breathe oxygen. Some lungfish have been known to live several years in this state! In amphibians like frogs, the young (tadpoles) have gills and the adults have lungs. Some salamanders (also amphibians), have both lungs and gills and can switch between them (or use them both) depending on the environmental conditions.

Reptiles, birds, and mammals all get their oxygen through lungs. **It is the swim bladder that evolved into lungs.** And that is why it is one of my "Big Moments in Animal Evolution."

Land Ho!

"I am a fish. But I want to live on land. What changes do I have to make?" You might think of things like

- Modified limbs and body systems
- Well-developed lungs
- Waterproof skin
- A way to regulate your body temperature
- A way to lay eggs on land without them drying out

You would be right. All those things need to happen.

So, why land?

If life was so great under the sea, why come onto land at all? Sponges, jellies, coral, rotifers, mollusks, and all the fish seem to have evolved pretty well under water, so why did the amphibians and reptiles evolutionarily go through all these changes?

Food.

There were a lot of plants and insects on land and no larger predators to eat them. In fact, insects and plants had the land to themselves for millions of years! They have evolved complex food webs, camouflage, and ways of behavior – so much so that flowering plants and insects simply cannot exist without each other.

There are millions of insects and plants on land. Fish, amphibians, and reptiles wanted to eat them! We see some fish jumping out of water to eat insects. The amphibians hopped onto land (*that's punny*). However, amphibians have to keep their skin moist and they have to go back to the water to lay their eggs, so they were still tied to the water.

Reptiles were the first group to make a **complete** transition to life on land. They do not have to keep their skin moist and they are able to lay their eggs on land. This was a major advancement in evolution. It leads us to the next topic, **the amniotic egg.**

The Amniotic Egg

Guess what?!? Your parents are sending you on spring break! There is a little catch. They can't really afford a plane ticket or car ride. They are going to pack you in a crate. "That's okay," you think. "I really want to go on spring break. Just make sure that it is a hard crate so that I don't get crushed. Also, I need to be able to breathe. And I need food. And water. I would also like a blanket and a way to get rid of waste material."

Meet the amniotic egg!

You are familiar with amniotic eggs. Chicken eggs (breakfast, anyone?) are amniotic eggs. All bird and reptile eggs are amniotic eggs. They have a hard shell, both for protection and for keeping water in. They contain the young animal, food, water, and a covering. They have small pores to let air in while keeping water from leaving. They are truly an engineering masterpiece! Life simply could have never taken hold on land without the amniotic egg!

Ectothermy and Endothermy

Another challenge to life on land is regulating your body temperature. In Colorado not long ago, the air temperature went from 102°F (39°C) to 27°F (3°C) in 24 hours! That is a lot of change! Living organisms on land need to be able to adapt to a rapidly changing temperature.

There are two main ways to do this; **ectothermy** and **endothermy.**

Ectothermy ("cold-blooded") is when organisms regulate their body temperature by using the external environment. When an animal is too cold, it may bask in the sun. When an animal is too warm, it may burrow in the mud or swim in water. Water is able to maintain a more consistent temperature than air. Reptiles, such as turtles and snakes, are ectothermic. Of course, a lot of ectothermic animals, such as lizards, live in environments that do not have extreme temperature changes. The tropics are a good example.

It is technically wrong to call amphibians and reptiles "cold-blooded" because their blood is not any colder than ours. It is the *way they maintain their heat* that is different.

The great advantage to ectothermy is that these animals do not have to eat as much as endothermic animals. Ectotherms can eat approximately 85% less food when heating their bodies.

Endothermy ("warm-blooded") is when organisms maintain a steady body temperature through their metabolism. This means that approximately 85% of the food they eat is burned through metabolism to heat the body. Birds and mammals, including humans, are endothermic.

Can you imagine being ectothermic? If you didn't have your heater on and your house got chilly, your parents would have to call you in late to school! "We're sorry, but Jimmy is too cold to move this morning. We put him on our heat rock and he will be back at school as soon as he heats up a little."

Also, 85% less food? This could be an advantage in solving world hunger, but I would sure miss taco day!

That's It!

So, there they are. The Big Moments in Animal Evolution including body cavities, the anus, the swim bladder, moving onto land, the amniotic egg, and endothermy. All small steps for individuals, but large steps for animal kind!

WITH GRATITUDE

I'd like to thank my students- my current students who gave me feedback on these stories and my past students who laughed with me and often moaned, "We don't get it!", therefore, making it necessary to make up these ridiculous stories. You, Students, have always been the inspiration.

I'd like to thank Justine, Chad, Karl, and the BHS faculty for the encouragement and patience in answering my many questions.

Savannah White is the amazing (student!) talent behind the interior graphics. Signe and Halle, thank you for the editing!

And...thank you! I sincerely hope these stories help to deepen your understanding of, and appreciation for, biology. And, I hope, that they made you laugh a little along the way. I'd love to hear your thoughts, comments, or ideas for new stories! Connect with me at:
https://heathermoran4.wixsite.com/biologyhelp

Made in the USA
Coppell, TX
20 September 2023

21760937R00085